HEITOR VILLA-LOBOS

Life and Work
of the Brazilian Composer

VASCO MARIZ

BRAZILIAN AMERICAN CULTURAL INSTITUTE. INC.
Washington, D.C.

To Therezinha, my wife

Foreword

IT IS A RARE PRIVILEGE to be able to present this timely and important study of the late great musical composer of Brazil, Heitor Villa-Lobos. The author, a musicologist and a diplomat, was a friend and admirer of his fellow countryman. As a musical historian Dr. Vasco Mariz has contributed several works on this phase of Brazilian culture, and his fame has extended to all parts ot the Western world. In a brief introduction, Dr. Gilbert Chase, a friend of the author and a musicologist himself, has set the background of Dr. Mariz' interests. Again a grant from the Pan American Foundation, Inc., has made possible the free distribution of this work to libraries and scholars.

A. CURTIS WILGUS, *Director*
School of Inter-American Studies

Introductory Note

WHEN I FIRST MET VASCO MARIZ—in 1953—we both belonged to that rare species, the musicologist-diplomat. He was at the time Brazilian consul in Rosario, Argentina, and I was cultural attaché of the American Embassy in Buenos Aires. Drawn together by our common predicament—for it is a predicament to be both a scholar and a diplomat—we soon became close friends; over the years I have scarcely known which to admire most: his professional *savoir-faire* as a diplomat (which in 1960 brought him to the post of counselor of embassy in Washington), his knack for picking winning horses at fantastic odds, or his very knowledgeable writings on music (he is also, by the way, an excellent singer, with considerable concert experience in his prediplomatic days). Reversing my own situation, he became a diplomat by profession and a musicologist by avocation; unlike myself, he managed to combine his profession and his avocation without excessive strain on either. While holding diplomatic appointments in Portugal, in Yugoslavia, in Argentina, in Italy, and, most recently, in the United States, Vasco Mariz was able to produce half a dozen books on musical subjects, of which the most important are *Figuras da Música Brasileira Contemporânea* (1948), *A Canção da Câmara no Brasil* (1948; later revised and enlarged as *A Canção Brasileira*, 1960), and, of course, the work of which the present monograph offers a condensed English version: *Heitor Villa Lobos, Compositor Brasileiro* (Rio de Janeiro, 1949).

At the time of his death in December, 1959, Heitor Villa-

Lobos had been the most famous composer of Latin America for at least three decades. He was one of the "revolutionary" artists who participated in the "Week of Modern Art" at São Paulo in 1922, helping to stir up a tempest of vituperation in the press. Yet today his delightful pieces for piano are as acceptable as the *Kinderszenen* of Schumann or the *Préludes* of Debussy, while some of his larger works, particularly certain of the *Chôros* and the *Bachianas Brasileiras,* already have the classical quality of enduring art.

With the passing of Villa-Lobos, the movement known as "Musical Nationalism" came to a close, or at least lost all of its *élan vital:* he was the last great representative of a trend—based on the use or adaptation of folk and popular elements to provide "local color"—that twentieth-century internationalism has made obsolete. And yet the nationalism of Villa-Lobos should not be exaggerated: Mariz calls him "compositor brasileiro," just as Debussy called himself "musicien français"; but today we know that the greatness of Debussy resides, not in his being French, but in his universality. In time to come, the best of Villa-Lobos' music will, I am certain, be no less universal in its appeal, while not ceasing to be one of the chief glories of Brazilian culture.

The republication of Dr. Vasco Mariz' authoritative monograph on Villa-Lobos, coinciding with the tenth anniversary of the composer's death, comes not only as a timely tribute but also a gratifying indication of continued interest in the United States for the life and work of the greatest Latin American composer of the first half of the twentieth century.

A decade is but the tenth part of a century, and even a century is but a short span of history in which to confer a title of immortality upon composers or artists whom we regard as great in our time. Perhaps in the new post-industrial era of rapid technical change and equally rapid obsolescence the only "Immortal Masters" will be those previously enshrined in the Museum (or should we say, Mausoleum?) of the Standard Repertory.

Yet when we consider how universally known some of Villa-Lobos' music has become in the decade since his death—for example the *Bachianas Brasileiras* No. 5, which has been interpreted by artists as different in background and style as Joan Baez and the Modern Jazz Quartet—then we are encouraged to believe that the music of the Brazilian master will long live not merely within the confines of the concert hall and the standard repertory, but also in the hearts and minds of many people in many walks of life, in many places of the world, and for many centuries to come.

GILBERT CHASE, *Director*
Inter-American Institute
for Musical Research

Introduction

THE BRAZILIAN PEOPLE have always been musical and the elements which formed their ethnic character
were, to a great extent, musical. Three races have contributed
to the formation of the Brazilian ethnic type: the white, the
black, and the red.

The white influence, namely that of the European contribution of Portuguese, Spanish, French, Italian, German, and
Polish immigrants, has undoubtedly been the most important
in music. "The Portuguese gave the Brazilians their harmonic
tonality, strophic quadrature, and probably syncopation also,
which was developed by contact with African rhythms."[1] The
instruments came from Portugal, the musical literature from
all over Europe. Spanish music has been influential through
boleros, fandangos, *seguidillas,* habaneras, and zarzuelas.
Spanish-American music has left traces too, first through the
pericón and, more recently, through the tango. One notices
a strong French influence in Brazilian children's songs, while
Italian opera has made a deep imprint since it came into
vogue in Brazil in the eighteenth century. Finally, the Aus-
trian waltz has been widely played, and in the last twenty
years American jazz has exerted a powerful influence, especially in the orchestration of Brazilian popular music.

From the last quarter of the sixteenth century until 1850,
the slave traffic brought in millions of black people who have
played a very significant role in the crystallization of the
Brazilian soul and ethnic type. In 1960, the population of

1. Mário de Andrade, *História da Música* (São Paulo), p. 185.

African origin still accounted for about 40 per cent of the Brazilian people, although the number of black citizens is being gradually reduced by frequent intermarriage. Their main musical contribution is rhythm. They have added sensuality to the Brazilian dance and introduced into it a dramatic or fetichistic character.

True aborigines, or Indians, in modern Brazil represent less than 1 per cent of the total population. Although their role has not been as significant as that of their North American counterparts, their influence should not be minimized. Since the sixteenth century, missionaries have exploited the Indian's inherent love of music, to the extent that Gregorian music has almost been forgotten by the superimposing of Christian texts on Indian melodies as a means for better teaching of the catechism.

Such significant contributions have perceptibly increased the Brazilian leaning toward music. All this varied and abundant material was to amalgamate and produce the first composed speciments of Brazilian music. Yet a true national music emerged in Brazil only with the appearance of Heitor Villa-Lobos, and this almost a century after the consecration of Glinka and Chopin. *Weltschmerz,* the longing for home, the simple pleasure of regional traditions, the glorification of the Indian (one hundred years after *Atala*), became part of Brazilian musical awareness in spite of the delay imposed by poor communications with Europe thousands of miles away.

In the last century in Brazil, the mere mention of an authentic Brazilian classical work or even the praising of popular music was cause for derision. Italian operatic music reigned unchallenged, in spite of some timid incursions by German or French masters. Talented Brazilian artists went to Europe for the perfecting of their skills and minimized the music of the slaves and the Indian melodies.

On March 5, 1887, the day Heitor Villa-Lobos was born in Rio de Janeiro, the exclusive patrons of the Beethoven Club and the Classical Concerts Society were paying homage to the "Fantasia for Piano" from Bellini's opera *Sonnambula,* applauding frenetically Milan's La Scala Opera Company, and listening to some of the Beethoven sonatas with obvious boredom.

Born in the second decade of the twentieth century, and more effective in orchestral and piano music than in opera, Brazilian national music has been interpreted by scholars as being superficial and descriptive. As one frequently comes across a composition of strong Negro or Indian character played as music representative of Brazil, this would seem to confirm this belief—a belief not uncommonly held to be true of countries, like Brazil, which in their own right are richly endowed with folk music. Instead, such music should be understood as a true expression of the Brazilian soul, of deep psychological growth, maturing through the centuries, and not solely as a depiction of the external manifestations of Brazilian life such as its dances, songs, street vendors' cries, etc. Music should represent more than momentary artistic amusement. It must inspire and arouse sublime esthetic emotion and not just impress the audience with this or that typical, colorful picture. Few composers have attained this level in national music. In Brazil, many are content just to adorn a folk musical cell with an erudite frame. Others drape it in fatuous and multicolored orchestrations, but very few have penetrated the *mare tenebrosum* of pure national music.

Villa-Lobos was the explorer of this domain in Brazil and the one who showed his contemporaries the right course through it. His works have easily surpassed the obvious stages of national music and often explore the spiritual depths of the Brazilian character. Villa-Lobos' works represent the solid foundation upon which the younger Brazilian composers are striving to build the monument to Brazilian folklore. Will they outdo Villa-Lobos?

Brazilian national music has had the special merit of revealing Brazil to its nationals. But it was a long fight. The best of Alberto Nepomuceno was not understood in his time. Musicians of outstanding talent were forced to disguise Brazilian national works under alien titles. Villa-Lobos was booed by the public and by the art critics. The "São Paulo

Week of Modern Art" of 1922 was a turning point in the suffocating European influence on Brazilian culture. It erased old prejudices and expedited a fair evaluation of Brazilian national art. Villa-Lobos played a significant role in this aggressive renovating cultural movement in Brazil, and his music has been considered an effective means for the imposition of modernistic ideas in his home country.

Villa-Lobos playing billiards

1 / Early Life

RIO DE JANEIRO at the turn of the century was still a long way from the bustling cosmopolitan metropolis that it is today. Then the capital of Brazil, it was a sleepy tropical city governed by an elite strongly influenced by European culture. Daily life moved at a slow pace, and in the evenings serenaders wandered through the streets courting their lovely *senhoritas*.

Heitor Villa-Lobos was born there on March 5, 1887.[1] His

---

1. The biographers of Villa-Lobos have variously dated his birth from 1881 to 1891. It is pertinent to quote an article published by Lisa Peppercorn in *Monthly Musical Record* (London, No. 898, July-August 1948), pp. 153-56, entitled "History of Villa-Lobos' Birthday Date." "The year of his birth was always a puzzle to everyone interested in the composer's art and the happenings of his life. It seems natural that Villa-Lobos himself ought to have known in which year he was born. However, he did not. Not that he ignored it entirely, but his statements as to the exact date varied according to the circumstances; possibly he did not even care in which year he was born. Lexicographers, musicologists, and others looking for facts, however, thought differently. Most, if not all, of them naturally turned to Villa-Lobos himself in the first place. Once such a date appeared in one or the other of the publications recognized in the musical world as reliable standard works; the date went on being quoted by others, with reference to the source of publication. It so happens that Grove's *Dictionary of Music and Musicians* (Supplementary Volume, London, 1940) and Baker's *Biographical Dictionary of Musicians* (Fourth edition, revised and enlarged, New York, 1940) both carry the date 1881. Renato Almeida, the Brazilian musicologist, must have been reluctant to accept this, for he chose his own sources and gave 1890 as the date of Villa-Lobos' year of birth in his *Historia da Música Brasileira* (Second edition, Rio de Janeiro, 1942), the standard book on Brazilian musical history. We had seen the same date in two publications that appeared in France about twenty years ago: a book entitled *Kings, Jazz and David* by Irving Schwerké (Paris, 1927) and an article in the French periodical *Musique* (No. 4, January 15, 1929) by Suzanne Demarquez. Both writers were in touch with Villa-Lobos during the composer's stay in France at that time, which leads to the assumption that it was Villa-Lobos himself who furnished the information. Andrade Muricy, a music critic of Rio de Janeiro's leading morning newspaper, *Jornal do Comercio*, who belongs to a group intimately connected with the composer's art choral singing and teaching, gives 1885 in a publication entitled *Musique Brésilienne Moderne* (Rio de Janeiro, 1937). And Prof. Luiz Heitor Correa de Azevedo, who holds the chair of folklore at the National School of Music at the University of Brazil in Rio de Janeiro, and who is well known both in Brazil and the United States for his reliable research work, agreed to 1885 in his *Relação*

parents lived on Ipiranga Street in the fashionable Flamengo Beach section. The child was born into a traditionally Brazilian home headed by a serious man, Raul Villa-Lobos, senior officer of the Brazilian National Library, a scholar, author of several publications on history and cosmography, and a good musician. Raul was a stern, energetic, and, at times, despotic father. He trained his son in musical theory so that at the age of 11, when his father died, Heitor could play the cello and clarinet.

His mother, Noêmia Monteiro Villa-Lobos, was not happy about the idea of Heitor becoming a musician. Her innermost desire for her "Tuhú," as he was nicknamed, was that he

---

das Operas de Autores Brasileiros (Rio de Janeiro, 1938). All of these writers accepted the date, from whatever source they got it, in good faith.

"Villa-Lobos' identity papers contain almost as great a variety of birth dates as he has documents. His French *carte d'identité* issued on December 15, 1927, bears the year 1891; his former voting paper, dated October 6, 1934, mentions 1883. In order to be safe from any further bother and, at the same time, to satisfy all those who were approaching him to clear up, once and for all, the mystery about the year of his birth, Villa-Lobos, in 1941, asked the editor of the musical periodical in Rio de Janeiro. *Musica Viva,* to include in a special issue dedicated to him (Ano I, No. 7/8, Jan./Feb. 1941) a summarized authentic biography which he himself supplied. He decided on this occasion to have been born in 1888. A few months later in the same year (1941) Nicolas Slonimsky was in Rio de Janeiro on his tour through South America. Not trusting anyone or anything that was said or published with regard to Villa-Lobos' birthdate, he heard from the composer (as the present writer, too, and doubtless many others had done) that Villa Lobos remembered he had been baptized in the Church of São José on the Rua Misericórdia in Rio de Janeiro. However, Slonimsky says in his book *Music of Latin America* (New York, 1945), that 'my diligent search in the Birth Registries of that church revealed no entry on Villa Lobos.'

"It would certainly be useless to undertake a search through birth registers, because during the period of the alleged years of Villa-Lobos' birth, that is from 1881 to 1891, birth registration was not compulsory in Brazil. When Villa-Lobos was married at the registrar's office on November 12, 1913, a birth certificate or anything stating the year of his birth was apparently not available, for the present writer found at the registrar's office that Villa-Lobos' mother made a statement (dated October 24, 1913) which was attached to the marriage documents, to be found at the Eighth Civil Registry in Rio de Janeiro, in which she declares that her son was born in the Federal Capital in 1886. (The marriage registration, however, says that Villa-Lobos was twenty-eight years old.) Yet even Villa-Lobos' mother was wrong as has now been proved. Vasco Mariz, who is working in the Brazilian Ministry of Foreign Affairs and preparing a little book on Villa-Lobos which will soon be published, may not have known about Slonimsky's pilgrimage to the São José church. Be that as it may, he paid a call at the same church and found Villa-Lobos was born on March 5, 1887. On the same day, Villa-Lobos' sister was baptized—Carmen, his junior by approximately one year and a half (born October 10, 1888)."

would become a physician. It was probably for this reason that she was opposed to his studying piano. When he was taking guitar lessons from a neighbor, he had to keep the fact hidden from his mother. She probably feared that if he became too enthusiastic about music, he would have neither the time nor the inclination to study medicine.

His early life was happy. His home was comfortable and he was loved by everyone. When he was 6, his father wrote a series of articles, carried by Rio newspapers, against the towering political personality of Brazil, Marshall Floriano Peixoto, and was advised to leave the capital for a while. So the Villa-Lobos family spent several months in the interior of Rio de Janeiro state, and later moved farther away to Bicas and Cataguazes, in the state of Minas Gerais. This enforced pilgrimage through the hinterland was young Heitor's first contact with rural music, which charmed him and made a definite imprint on his mind. The "hillbilly" songs delighted him, and he plunged deeper and deeper into Brazilian folk music, which he was much later to bring to the attention of the world.

When the family returned to Rio, he continued to study cello with his father on a specially adapted viola. He improvised simple melodies based on the children's songs he learned from young street companions. None of his brothers showed any interest in music in spite of the paternal influence. Their aunt Zizinha, however, was a good pianist and especially fond of Bach. This seems to have been his first acquaintance with the Eisenach genius: an influence that was to become a lasting one, as we shall see when commenting on the series of *Brazilian Bachianas*. Heitor's grandfather, Santos Monteiro, was also an amateur musician and the author of a well-known quadrille of his time.

When Raul Villa-Lobos moved back to the capital he found a new home on Riachuelo Street in the downtown area. Every Saturday evening at eight o'clock, the Villa-Lobos family and several friends would gather regularly for an evening of chamber music, playing until the early hours of the morning. Even the Vice-President of the Republic,

Manuel Vitorino, would come to these musical *soirées* to which young Heitor listened attentively from the top of the stairs. On other occasions, his father would take him to visit a friend who was an authority on the folk music of the Northeast of Brazil. He met there some of the most famous popular singers and serenaders who added much to the fascination that folk songs had acquired for him during his stay in the hinterland states.

Raul Villa-Lobos died in 1899, leaving his family in financial difficulties, and Noêmia had a hard struggle to bring up their children. A good friend obtained a job for young Heitor as office boy but it did not last long. His association with popular musicians had always been resented by his parents, but now he felt free to approach his idols, and the means were at hand. His father left a valuable library and young Heitor had discovered that some of the precious books could be sold to book shops for considerable amounts of money. Thereafter, diplomatic relations with popular singers and players expanded, thanks to drinks financed at appropriate times by the would-be composer.

Rio, at the turn of the century, was proud of the *chôro*. Groups of young men would form instrumental bands, playing at parties, balls, marriages, celebrations, and Carnival, continuing their playing in the streets after the close of the events. As crowds followed them asking for encores, they played, sometimes throughout the entire night, with short interruptions at the nearest bar for a stimulating drink. Different groups would meet in the winding streets and challenge each other to musical competition, which more than once ended in a fist fight. In Rio then one could not imagine the moon high in the sky without the serenaders, the *chorões*, the plaintive guitar, and the folk songs. The musicians walked mile after mile, all night long, singing and playing just for the pleasure of it.

There is, however, a difference between the simple serenaders and the *chorões*. The serenade featured a vocalist accompanied by an instrumental ensemble very much in the traditional Spanish manner. In the *chôro* the human voice is rarely present. The instrumentalists created music, they improvised melodies or variations, and they produced beautiful harmonies in a spontaneous and fluent original ensemble. The *chôro* is essentially *carioca,* that is, native to Rio. Originally, the name *chôro* identified a kind of music from the Cidade Nova (new city) area; but by the middle of the last century the name was extended to musicians from the entire city of Rio. Such music is usually gay and lively. "Tico-Tico," although written much later, is a good example of *chôro* music with which the American public is becoming familiar.

Another distinction should be made here: the *chorão* has a deep feeling for the spontaneity of his creation. He would surrender his soul when playing. It was to him a cult, a religion. The *chorão* lived to play, to compose, and to sing. Love affairs were mere incidents. The man who would try to serenade an attractive woman was never considered a *chorão*. Singers were also rare, as I have mentioned before. Only the famous Eduardo das Neves and Catulo were accepted as part of the *chorões* groups.

The musicologist Correa de Azevedo, in comparing the music of *chorões* with the jam sessions of American jazz, remarked that although improvisation was common to both instrumental groups, the *chôro* music used to require virtuoso ability to perform it, while the jam session music is richer in harmony and orchestral color. The *chôro* improvisation was stressed in an instrumental solo with its modulations, while at jam sessions there is improvisation of several instruments successively or concurrently.

As Villa-Lobos grew up, he became a member of the group directed by Quincas Laranjeira, which used to meet at the "Cavaquinho de Ouro" on Carioca Street. Some of its members—Anacleto de Medeiros, Irinen de Almeida, Luiz Gonzaga da Hora, Juca Kalu, and Zé do Cavaquinho—became justly famous. Young Heitor played the guitar and the influence of these times is perceived in the first Brazilian Bachiana, whose fugue was composed very much in the style of Sátiro Bilhar, another popular player.

2 / The Rebel

VILLA-LOBOS' works came out of a strenuous and often difficult life. As a young man he knew the pangs of hunger many times, and for several years led a precarious life as a player in a modest popular band. He traveled through Brazil under conditions of extreme discomfort, knew the isolation of living abroad with few friends, and encountered tenacious opposition from art critics and the general public for many years. All of this must have tempered his talent and perhaps hardened his soul in his last days. He made an early effort or two at conventional endeavor: he finished high school at São Bento in spite of his great enthusiasm for the *chorões,* and tried to fulfil his mother's wishes that he become a medical doctor, but after a few months of classes, he gave up. At the age of 16 he left home to live with his Aunt Zizinha in order to escape his mother's reprimands about his disorganized life. It was the beginning of a painful Bohemian way of living which lasted for several years. He played in night clubs, hotels, movie theaters, bars. At the Recreio Theater, the most popular in Rio at the time, he was a cellist in the orchestra, where he played operas, operettas, and zarzuelas. His compositions at this time were still modest, limited to waltzes, schottisches, military marches, polkas, and the like. He met the most renowned popular artists of his time and absorbed their art and style in such a manner that much later it would return to his mind and be expressed in his works with spontaneous, authentic color.

When he was 18, he was seized with the desire to discover the country, sold the rest of the fine books his father had left him to finance the trip, and visited the states of Espírito Santo, Bahia, and Pernambuco. The old colonial cities of

Salvador and Recife charmed him, and he spent several months there holding part-time jobs. He went farther into the hinterland of the Northeastern states and studied the music of popular singers *in situ,* their style of interpretation and their primitive instruments. In a self-invented shorthand he recorded the cowboys' calls and chants, the *desafios* (musical duels of improvisations between two singers), the popular *autos* (short plays), and dramatic dances. All these interested him deeply and evoked the strong national feeling which he would demonstrate in his classical works. In his several trips throughout Brazil, he eventually collected over one thousand musical themes and rhythms.

After these first months of wandering in the Northeast, Villa-Lobos returned to Rio and began composing songs and fantasies for solo guitar. He was 20 when he accepted an invitation from a friend to visit Southern Brazil and work at a match factory in Paranaguá, Paraná, where he fell in love with the owner's daughter and almost married her. But as far as his music was concerned, his stay was disappointing. This section of the country is heavily infiltrated by European immigrants and so close to the Argentine border that the folk music he could collect there was hardly original and of little scientific interest. Therefore, in spite of the tempting offer to join a rich family by marriage, he felt he should continue his pilgrimage. He left Paranaguá as Bach had left Hamburg after a short idyll with Buxtehude's daughter.

In 1907 Villa-Lobos was again in Rio, where he registered at the National Institute of Music for the class in harmony. He took lessons with Agnelo França, a composer, but found the severe teaching of Frederico Nascimento too restraining. He could never adjust himself to routine methods although he respected his teacher and another composer, Francisco Braga, the only musicians who gave him advice about the kind of music he was trying to write. *Cánticos Sertanejos* date from this period and represent his first experiment in the utilization of regional musical themes for small orchestra.

His association with Nascimento did not last long: a few

months later he was again on the roads of Brazil, this time going westward to the states of São Paulo, Mato Grosso, and Goiás. Back in Rio, he started out on a fourth trip, his second to the Northeast, which even today offers the best possibilities for folklore studies in Brazil. This time he traveled with a companion known by the rather surprising name of Donizetti. They would play in every little town, collect the meager results, and proceed to the next engagement. In one place there was a rivalry between two villages because of a military march. The mayors of both towns were trying in vain to steal each other's tune when Villa-Lobos visited their towns. Unknown in that area, he attended a rehearsal, took down the music without any mistakes and sold it to the mayor of the other town for a considerable sum of money. He became the hero of that village, but soon had to flee the state because the victims of his ruse were threatening to kill him!

In the state of Acre in the Amazon region, Villa-Lobos contracted malaria and had to fight it for several weeks. He met different tribes of Indians but never ran into cannibals. Later, in Bahia, he heard for the first time some compositions by a French musician named Debussy. They did not impress him very much, perhaps because they were badly interpreted by the performer; it took Artur Rubinstein himself, years later, to reveal to Villa-Lobos all the secrets of his seductive music, which was to influence his works so strongly in a certain period of his life.

When he returned to Rio, he was surprised to learn that his mother, believing him dead, had ordered a mass to be said in his memory. At this time, he wrote two one-act operas, *Aglaia* and *Eliza*. Later, from January to May of 1912, he composed the opera *Izaht* in four acts—a sort of fusion and expansion of the previous two. Other compositions of this time were the *Double String Quintet*, works for violin and piano, and songs and religious choruses for the St. Cecilia School, which was then directed by his friend, Father Alpheu. At this period he became fascinated with the works of Wagner and Puccini. *Tristan* was cause for ecstasy, and one notes in the operas mentioned above traces of Wagnerian orchestration methods and motifs of Puccinian melodies. This was, however, a transitory influence; as the composer himself once told me, "As soon as I feel someone's influence on me, I shake myself and jump out of it."

A more lasting impression may have been the careful reading of Vincent d'Indy's *Cours de Composition Musicale.* We should bear in mind that Brazil, at the turn of the century, was under a tight French cultural grip which was to last almost until the Second World War. Young Heitor had been able to read French since he was a teen-ager, and it seems that he could actually speak the language with some fluency when he was 21. D'Indy's technical influence is traceable in Villa-Lobo's first two symphonies, in the *Sonata No. 2* for cello and in the trios (with the exception of the *Trio No. 1).*

By now, we have established the fact that as far as the routine learning of music and routine living were concerned, Villa-Lobos was a nonconformist. In 1915 the first concerts of his works showed a series of musical innovations still unfamiliar to Brazilian music lovers, which encountered strong resistance from the art critics, thus suffocating public opinion. It seems that Villa-Lobos had not yet studied recent works by Schoenberg and Stravinsky, who were becoming so well known in Paris, thanks to their daring and unusual harmonic methods. His experiments may be considered spontaneous and original, although still a long way from the magnificent blossoming of his talent, awakened by the knowledge of the young and brilliant European masters later revealed to him.

On November 13, 1915, he started a series of concerts at the *Jornal de Comercio* hall. The *Trio No. 1,* the *Sonata No. 2,* the *Waltz Scherzo* for piano solo, a *Berceuse* for cello and piano, and several songs were performed with controversial results. Special resistance came from the art critic Oscar Guanabarino, who fought Villa-Lobos until his death in 1936.[1] Such resistance to his works was not limited to the

---

1. A good example of art critic Oscar Guanabarino's attacks on Villa-Lobos is the following: "Such an artist cannot be understood by musicians simply because

critics and the general public. The musicians in the orchestras which had to play his music also seethed with rebellious indignation. In 1918, when preparing the National Institute of Music orchestra for a concert of his music, Villa-Lobos had a hard time convincing the *spala* to play his symphonic poem *Amazon*, and with other groups of musicians who refused to try his First Symphony, both of which are considered moderate today.

Nevertheless, he was not unsupported. The well-known art critic, Rodrigues Barbosa, and the writers, Coelho Neto, Ronald de Carvalho, and Renato Almeida, as well as the best performing artists of his time, were campaigning strongly in his favor. At this time, the music of Villa-Lobos had already crossed the borders of Brazil. The prestigious Wagnerian Association of Buenos Aires had welcomed his *String Quartet, Opus 15,* and in Rio, maestro Gino Marinuzzi included the adagio and the scherzo of his First Symphony in a concert at the opera house. It was the beginning of an international vogue which now extends to every corner of the world.

Villa-Lobos was still earning his living as a cello player but turning more and more to composing. The two ballets, *Amazon* and *Uirapurú*, the piano suite *The Baby's Family No. 1,* and the *Chôro No. 1* are some of the works written at this time which are familiar to music lovers.

A little earlier, in 1917, the young composer had been introduced to a Frenchman of about his age, Darius Milhaud, then secretary to Paul Claudel at the French Legation

---

he does not understand himself in the delirium of his productive fever. His works are incoherent, full of musical cacophonies, and a conglomeration of musical notes without connection. What he wants to do is fill music sheets and the number of his compositions should be figured by net weight, in tons, without a single page destined to come out of a maelstrom of vulgarity. Mr. Villa Lobos, who is still young, has written much more than any true and active composer could have written during his lifetime. His motto is not to write 'little and well' but 'much' even if it is no good at all. The public did not understand Villa Lobos's Frenetic Dance because it bears a wrong title, which should be St. Vitus' Dance with an explanatory note advising that it should be performed by epileptic musicians and heard by paranoiacs" *(Jornal do Comercio)*.

in Rio. He first resented the critical temperament of the musician-diplomat, but soon they became good friends and Villa-Lobos acquainted him with the music of Rio, introducing him to the *chorões* and carnival music, and explaining to him the *macumba* fetichist rites. The famous Milhaud suites *Saudades do Brasil* and *Scaramouche* contain many reminiscences of his stay in Rio.

Curiously enough, it was in Oporto, Portugal, in 1948 that I had occasion to meet two good Parisian friends of Villa-Lobos—Artur Rubinstein, the famous pianist, and Marius-François Gaillard, the able French conductor. The virtuoso recalled happily the time he was in Buenos Aires and ready to leave for Brazil when the conductor Ernst Ansermet advised him to meet an extraordinary musician in Rio who was capable of playing any modern work. In Rio, he was introduced to the Brazilian pianist, Henrique Oswald, but he soon realized that this was not the man he was looking for. At a party, Rubinstein met young Darius Milhaud and he thought the mystery was solved as the Frenchman was also the dark-skinned Brazilian type. Later, the pianist went to a movie theater and there, by chance, heard a modest orchestra playing some strange and unusual music. He approached the author to congratulate him, but Villa-Lobos repelled the gesture by saying, "You are a virtuoso. You cannot understand my music!"

The next morning, to Rubinstein's astonishment, the Brazilian composer and a dozen other musicians invaded his hotel room. He apologized for his rudeness of the previous evening and said he had asked some friends who worked in the afternoon and evening to come with him to play for Rubinstein. It was the beginning of a lasting and profitable friendship. The great pianist has been a champion of Villa-Lobos' music and has made several recordings of it. The *Rude Poema* for piano solo is dedicated to him. In 1941, at the request of Nelson Rockefeller, Rubinstein gave an entire concert of Villa-Lobos' works at the New York Museum of Modern Art during the Cândido Portinari exhibit there.

In order to help Villa-Lobos financially, when things went

wrong in Paris, Rubinstein invented a hypothetical collector and bought from him the autographed manuscript of his cello sonata at a very high price. Years later, Villa-Lobos found these originals by chance at the virtuoso's home. It was also Rubinstein who urged Carlos Guinle, the Brazilian industrialist, to sponsor Villa-Lobos' trip to Europe and the publishing of some of his best works in Paris. Rubinstein had some reservations about the unevenness of Villa-Lobos' musical production as a whole, but he told me in Portugal, "In spite of that, he is the most remarkable musician in the Americas."

A turning point in the updating of the music of Brazil was the "Week of Modern Art," which took place in São Paulo in February, 1922. Villa-Lobos first heard of so ambitious a project through the writers Graça Aranha and Ronald de Carvalho, who asked for his cooperation. He composed a few songs especially for it and organized the general musical program. There was serious opposition to "The Week" and the conservatives attended the three sessions at the opera house firmly disposed to deride the efforts of the young contributing artists. There were exhibits of paintings and sculpture at the theater hall and lectures and concerts on the stage.

The public's attitude toward Villa-Lobos was at first respectful but they soon began to boo and heckle the performing artists. One man brought a flute and at the end of each important melody he would try to imitate it. The shoulder strap of the violinist Paulina d'Ambrosio kept slipping down and someone from the gallery would yell, "Hold that strap." Paulina was shaking, and at the end of the sonata she burst into tears in front of the public. Baritone Nascimento Filho was ending a song in pianissimo when someone shouted the first words of *Pagliacci*'s prologue "Si può!" The singer lost his temper and invited the public to fight him on the street. The next day he appeared with a black eye. When Villa-Lobos, who had recently hurt one foot, came to the concerts wearing one shoe and one slipper, the public imitated his limping by noisily keeping time to his step. Pianist Guiomar

Novaes contributed her prestige to the historic experiment as one of the performers.

The Rio and São Paulo press either highly praised or harshly criticized the "Week of Modern Art." The publicity it received transformed a minor artistic quarrel into a theme for national debate. Newspapers, magazines, and publishers welcomed the controversy and with the passage of time the heroes of that week gained recognition.

Reception at the Waldorf Astoria in 1944.
From left, Villa-Lobos, Agent Leiser and
singer Marion Anderson

3 / Maturity

ARTUR RUBINSTEIN and the well-known *lieder* singer Vera Janacopulos were among the friends who encouraged Villa-Lobos to visit Europe. The music world of Rio de Janeiro was divided for and against the trip. Surprisingly enough, his archenemy, the art critic Guanabarino, supported the idea. Brazil's music dictator of those times, composer Francisco Braga, Villa-Lobos' ex-teacher, signed before a notary public a strange certificate of artistic competence:

> Mr. Heitor Villa-Lobos has enormous musical talent. He has shown amazing productive capacity and already possesses a remarkable artistic estate where one may find valuable works, some of them quite original. He is no longer a promise, he is an affirmation. I think Brazil will some day be proud of his son.
>
> December 5, 1920.
> (signed) Francisco Braga

> (Filed by notary Roquette, 116 Rosario Street, Rio de Janeiro)

Villa-Lobos' musical colleagues could not swallow this easily and published scathing articles about him in the Rio newspapers. There was a clipping entitled, "What a Profitable Business!" In spite of this adverse criticism, a draft bill was submitted to the Brazilian Congress granting Villa-Lobos the sum of 108 *contos* (approximately $10,000) for organizing and performing concerts of Brazilian music in Europe. There was bitter debate on the subject in the House of Representatives, but thanks to the brilliant support of the now famous writer Gilberto Amado the Brazilian government granted him 40 *contos* for this purpose.

In order to justify morally the sponsorship he had been given by Congress, Villa-Lobos conducted a series of four concerts devoted exclusively to his music at the Rio opera house. The public was indifferent, and the art critic Ronald de Carvalho wrote, "Villa Lobos; admirable effort was useless because he was not born by the Volga River and named Villiaff-Loboff, as well as the fact that he had not been engaged by impresario Mocchi [famous manager of the opera house at that time] to be the exotic personality of the season."

In the summer of 1923, Heitor Villa-Lobos left Rio on a French ship for Paris. He was not going to France to study but to show what he had accomplished. He was to benefit very much from the artistic atmosphere of Paris and eventually win his place in the sun there, but it took him many months to adapt himself to the new environment. He was fortunate in finding many friends who gave him a helping hand into the sophisticated world of music. Again Rubinstein came to his assistance by introducing him to the publisher Max Eschig and by playing his music on concert tours. Vera Janacopulos did the same. Florent Schmitt, Paul Le Flem, and Tristan Klingsor, important music critics, were sympathetic to his works. However, Villa-Lobos did not become widely known in Paris until the appearance of a controversial article in the newspaper *Intransigeant.*

He was preparing his works for a concert at the Salle Gaveau when the poetess and journalist Lucille Delarue Mardrus, a friend of the family, came across the book *Voyage to Brazil,* written by Hans Staden, a German traveler of the seventeenth century. She borrowed it and took it home. Days later, the newspaper published a sensational and exciting article in which it attributed to Villa-Lobos most of the adventures Staden had experienced three centuries before! He was supposed to have been a member of a German scientific expedition which was captured by cannibals and to have soothed them by playing records on a phonograph. Members of the Paris Brazilian colony were so outraged they even shunned him on the streets. He tried in vain to deny the story and swore to me that he had nothing to do with it, but he did admit that it helped him considerably by attracting a large crowd to the concert.

He was soon accepted in the innermost circle of the French capital's musical group. He was friendly with Florent Schmitt, Edgard Varèse, Pablo Picasso, Fernand Léger, the painter Roca (who did an excellent portrait of him playing the cello), Leopold Stokowski, and several other personalities of the times. Madame Penteado of São Paulo had helped him furnish an attractive house in Paris, and Isidor Phillip and Marguerite Long sent him pupils who were to study his music. Roger-Ducasse made him a professor of composition at the International Conservatory of Music in Paris, and he had occasion to play and conduct concerts in London, Amsterdam, Vienna, Berlin, Brussels, Madrid, Liège, Lyon, Amiens, Poitiers, Barcelona, and Lisbon.

In Paris, Villa-Lobos also met the famous composer and professor, Vincent d'Indy, who was complimentary about the new artistic contribution he had brought to France. The composer of *Istar* examined with care several of Villa-Lobos' works and suggested changes in the Third and Fourth Symphonies.

In May 1924, Villa-Lobos organized his first concert in Paris, with the assistance of the publisher Max Eschig. The site was the Salle des Agriculteurs. Cahuzac, the clarinetist, Louis Fleury, flautist, the bassoonist Dherin and Marcel Mule, saxophonist, took part in this Chamber Music Concert, conducted by the composer. The public, finding the music too daring for the times, reacted badly; but Villa-Lobos had attracted the attention of Jean Wiener who engaged him for a series of avant-garde concerts, together with other musicians who have since become celebrated.

Three years later, on October 24 and December 5, Villa-Lobos offered two more concerts with first performances of several *Choros, Rude poema* (composed for his friend Rubinstein), the *Serestas* and *Noneto*. These performances took place at the Salle Gaveau with the participation of the Orchestre Colonne, Artur Rubinstein (who still often performs the first Suite of *The Baby's Family*), Vera Janacopulos, Aline Van Barentzen, the Spanish pianist Thomas Terán and the French violinist Darrieux. The 250 voice group of "l'Art Choral" under the direction of Robert Siohan interpreted the mighty Choro No. 10. The Parisian press was highly laudatory.

This was the moment of consecration. From this time forward, Villa-Lobos had achieved fame in Paris and in the international music world. Maurice Raskin, moreover, recently told me in Brussels, as he recalled the pleasant evenings at Place Saint-Michel nearly thirty years ago, that the Brazilian musician had made a strong impression on the Paris musical world. They sensed in Villa-Lobos a new force, an original contribution to musical aesthetics, which exerted an attraction upon both composers and interpreters. Rarely could one attend the Soirées Musicales of Villa-Lobos without meeting a celebrated personality of contemporary music. According to the composer himself, the year 1927 was decisive in the promotion of his work and in obtaining the recognition of the great conductors.

Notwithstanding this success, his financial difficulties persisted. The reviews of Florent Schmitt, Paul le Flem, Tristan Klingsor, Rene Dumesnil and others, so full of enthusiasm, honored him greatly, but he was obliged to undertake burdensome labors editing music at Max Eschig's and to give numerous private lessons in order to better balance his modest budget.

One day, at the home of Prokofieff, he met Diaghilev, who was impressed by his music. Everything was prepared for the choreographing of the *Cirandas* and the *Suite No. 1* of *The Baby's Family* but the great Russian impresario died soon after.

He was an editor for music publisher Max Eschig, and when Roger Ducasse was appointed Director of the Paris International Conservatory,[1] he appointed Villa-Lobos Pro-

1. His colleagues on the Honorary Board were: Paul Dukas, Roger Ducasse, Gabriel Pierné, Maurice Ravel, Albert Roussel, Florent Schmitt, Alfred Casella,

fessor of Composition. At that time, Isidor Phillip and Marguerite Long were referring several students to him.

But the reader should not make the error of thinking that the works of Villa-Lobos had been accepted at first blush. The elite applauded him, and he enjoyed the esteem of informed music lovers, but detractors were not lacking: those very same people who raised such an outcry against French avant-grade artists. In 1930, a part of the public still displayed a total incomprehension towards this music, witness the following passage excerpted from a newspaper of the period:

"At the end of yesterday's concert, 'chez Lamoureux,' certain virtuosos of the whistle, endowed with uncommon pulmonary vigor, showed their disgust for the *Chôros* of M. Villa-Lobos. What a tumult. . . . For a quarter hour, members of the audience bellowed invective at one another. . . ." [2]

After his definitive return to Rio in 1930, and up until the year of his death in 1959, Villa-Lobos often journeyed to France to give concerts and for brief visits. The Marietti Brothers, who head the Max Eschig Publishing House, recall with warmth his frequent visits to 30, Rue de Rome. He never announced his arrival in advance by letter or cable, but was recognized, as he reached the foot of the stairs, simply by the odor of his cigar, to the elation of his publishers who remember him with affection. He would arrive with new works to be published; and correct the proofs of other works left during his last visit, all the while telling jokes or indulging in the latest Paris musical gossip. His popularity with his French publishers is apparent. Besides, the French always accorded him esteem, sympathy and respect. After the catcalls of 1924, he had rapidly achieved a growing success, already noticeable in 1927, which subsequently grew with his concerts in 1929, 1930 and with the presentation of *Chôro No. 10* as a ballet, at Salle Pleyel, in 1934 with Serge Lifar. Villa-Lobos, who nurtured a deep love towards France and

Manuel de Falla, Arthur Honegger, Joaquin Nin, Karol Szymanowski, Alberto Williams, Jose Iturbi, Arthur Rubinstein, Ricardo Viñes, Leo-Pol Morin, Aline Van Barentzen, René Dommange, Yves Nat, Jane Mortier and Albert Falcon.
2. R. Dezarneaux.—*La Liberte* (1930)

Paris, reciprocated the friendship of the French concertgoers, for he was proud to have awakened the interest and admiration of an audience so exacting as the Paris public.[3]

From 1926 to 1930, Villa-Lobos returned several times to Brazil to conduct concerts in Rio and especially in São Paulo, where he had the fianancial support of Madame Penteado and where he conducted the first performances in Brazil of important works by Honegger, Roussel, Poulenc, Ravel, and Florent Schmitt. In 1926, he directed three symphonic concerts at the Wagnerian Association of Buenos Aires and spent an invigorating vacation in Dakar at a friend's home there.

It should be remembered that this period in his life was one of prolific and inspired production: some authors consider it the most significant of his career. He was singularly fortunate in that he was able to enjoy long periods of happiness and self-affirmation, and the success of most of his works inspired him to greater artistic achievement. In this period between 1922 and 1930, he wrote the long and important series of *Chôros,* the *Cirandas* for piano solo, the excellent *Noneto* for chamber orchestra, *Momo Precoce* for piano and orchestra, Artur Rubinstein's *Rude Poema* and the well-known *Serestas* for voice and orchestra.

When he left Paris in 1930 for a series of concerts in Rio and São Paulo, Villa-Lobos could not have foreseen that he was destined to remain in Brazil for a long time. He organized a concert of his works in Recife, Pernambuco. Later he traveled to São Paulo, which was fast becoming a center

3. Here are four appropriate quotes which attest to the esteem he enjoyed in France:

"Villa-Lobos is loyal to Paris and Paris returns it in kind." (René Dumesnil, Le Monde, 3-9-1951.)

"Villa-Lobos, unknown to Paris music-lovers? Hardly. The Brazilian from Rio could claim among us honorary citizenship." (Paul le Flem, *Rolet,* 5-15-52.)

"Heitor Villa-Lobos has returned. The aura of musical renewal in Paris would lack luster if he were not to bring us, in addition to his presence, some evidence of his fecund personality." (René Dumesnil, *Le Monde,* 3-31-53).

"He loved the French ambiance. He has inhaled it too long to be able to deprive himself of its sweetness. But this does not alter his music in its essence." (Paul le Flem, *Rolet,* 4-29-54.).

of dangerous political activity. The musical season was seriously affected by the prevalent political unrest and Villa-Lobos planned to return earlier to Paris since he could not resume his concerts. In the meantime, struck by the lack of musical activities in Brazilian schools, he decided to draft a plan of music education to be submitted to the secretary of education of the state of São Paulo. Julio Prestes, a candidate for the Presidency of the Republic, had studied this plan at the home of Olivia Penteado and pledged to support it if he were elected.

The revolution was successful and Getulio Vargas was installed in the presidential palace in Rio, but Villa-Lobos was disappointed and ready to take the first ship back to Europe. Unexpectedly, he was summoned to the governor's mansion in São Paulo where he met Colonel João Alberto Lins de Barros, who was to be his friend and protector for many years. They soon reached an agreement and Villa-Lobos abandoned the idea of returning to Paris and plunged enthusiastically into his plan for music education. He traveled through the interior of São Paulo state for about two years introducing and supervising his project.

In 1932 he returned to Rio and founded the SEMA (Superintendency of Musical and Artistic Education). Villa-Lobos was active in many fields of education and even founded an orchestra bearing his name, which, unfortunately, did not last long. Professor Anisio Teixeira, a prominent member of the Ministry of Education, had supported Villa-Lobos' plan for several years, and it was through his influence that the study of orpheonic (choral) singing was fostered in the schools. A Professors' Choir was created which gave many well-attended and worth-while concerts. Villa-Lobos conducted stadium concerts of 18,000 voices in 1932 and of 30,000 voices with the participation of almost 1,000 musicians in 1935 and again in 1937. In 1942 he directed choirs of 40,000 students.

The educational activities of SEMA proceeded intensively until the creation of the National Conservatory for Orpheonic Singing on November 26, 1942, under the provisions of Public Law 4993. For several years Villa-Lobos was so indefatigable in organizing music teaching in Brazilian schools, in stimulating musicological research, and in recording Brazilian music that his educational work in Brazil is still highly regarded and deserving of the respect and appreciation of all music lovers. He promoted several series of youth concerts and left a valuable contribution to Brazilian folk music in his *Guia Pratico* ("Practical Guide"), consisting of six volumes, some of which have not yet been published.

It is pertinent to mention here Villa-Lobos' effort to improve the singing of the Brazilian national anthem. Regional influences and the average student's imperfect knowledge of pitch produced numerous and lasting mistakes in the interpretation of the beautiful anthem written by Francisco Manuel da Silva. Villa-Lobos decided to appoint a special committee to check these errors and distortions and issued an official directive suspending the singing of the anthem until a model interpretation had been agreed upon. This, needless to say, gave his enemies the opportunity they had been waiting for, and touched off further fiery criticism of the composer. They accused him of despising the national anthem, of wanting to introduce into it some of his own modernistic ideas, and even of wanting to substitute it with a work of his own.

The committee, consisting of composer Francisco Braga, Villa-Lobos himself, art critic Andrade Muricy, and the poets Olegario Mariano and Manuel Bandeira, counted fifty-nine mistakes in the usual interpretation of the anthem (twenty-seven rhythmic errors and thirty-two errors of intonation). The debate was long and acrimonious. It was finally resolved by Government Decree No. 5545 on July 31, 1942, with a clear victory for Villa-Lobos.

In 1934 Villa-Lobos returned to Paris for a short time to conduct the first performance of his ballet *Jurupary (Chôro No. 10)* at the Salle Pleyel on March 17, 1934, with dancer Serge Lifar in the title role. It was a remarkable success. In the same year he went to Buenos Aires for a series of three concerts. There he also conducted Bach's *Mass in B Minor*. In 1936 he represented Brazil at the Music Education Congress in Prague and was a member of the panel of judges in an international competition for pianists and singers in Vienna.

When he returned to Brazil he conducted concerts of his own music and important works such as Handel's *Judas Maccabeus* oratorio. He also gave much time and effort to the revival of folk dances of his homeland. In 1940 he visited Montevideo on a cultural mission, directed two concerts, and lectured on Brazilian music. Later in the year, when Leopold Stokowski and the All-American Youth Orchestra paid a visit to Brazil, Villa-Lobos was their host. He organized several concerts for them and favored their recording of Brazilian popular music which some authorities were reluctant to approve.

In 1943 he came to the United States for the first time and received the honorary degree of Doctor of Music at New York University. At the invitation of Serge Koussevitsky he later toured the United States and directed some of its best orchestras, including those of Boston and Philadelphia. After he returned to Brazil he again visited Argentina and toured Chile for the first time. In 1947 he went back to the United States for a second tour and received an honorary degree at Occidental College in Los Angeles. His comic opera, *Magdalena,* was performed in New York and Los Angeles with moderate success. In 1948 he was elected a corresponding member of the Institute of France, replacing Manuel de Falla.

Here is a characteristic comment from the Paris press. "Villa-Lobos' contribution has since changed. In the past, certain of his works have unleashed among us unforgettable clamor, at Salle Gaveau, this very hall. The powerful and captivating personality of Villa-Lobos is no less delightful, is not impaired by time; his music is hard, often brutal, with vivid scaffolding, and extremely violent colors. It often possesses an extraordinary density of sounds and draws impressive effect from Brazilian folklore. This kind of music is nonetheless his own, and remains, despite its exoticism, on the level of pure art." (Raymond Charpentier, *Arts,* 3-26-48.)

The second and third quarters of 1948 were most difficult

periods in the life of Villa-Lobos. He fell victim at that time to the first crisis which troubled his health and which was to prove fatal twelve years later. It was necessary to take urgent measures, and his doctor recommended an immediate trip to the United States, where he might take advantage of recent medical advances. His financial situation was far from satisfactory, but thanks to the aid of several friends, among whom the composer Oscar Lorenzo Fernandez, and of the Brazilian Government, he was able to make the trip to the United States. He entered Memorial Hospital in New York on July 9. His condition was considered serious, but he had at hand the friendship and the admiration of his Brazilian and American friends. A successful operation restored his enormous energy and vitality nearly completely although he was obliged thereafter to accept a slower pace in his musical activities. Some musicologists consider this date a confine in the creative life of Villa-Lobos. Time alone will give us the necessary perspective to render a judgment on this question.

Starting in 1949, Villa-Lobos was to make several tours. He traveled to Europe, the United States and even to Israel, where he composed a Symphonic Poem in homage to the new State. On March 17, 1949, René Dumesnil (*Le Monde)* gives us a glimpse of the composer's vitality: "Heitor Villa-Lobos has this week once again played a major role in the musical life of Paris." Soon afterward, Villa-Lobos was in Rome conducting a first reading of his Second Symphony at the Academy of St. Cecilia. In Paris, on the occasion of the fiftieth anniversary of his career in music, in March 1952, M. Louis Joxe, Minister of Education, presented him, during a private ceremony, an elaborate medal engraved by Mme. Coeffin and struck at the mint. In 1952, the State Government of São Paulo, Brazil, commissioned an important work from him on the occasion of the city's fourth Centennial; this was to be his *Symphony No. 10,* in five parts, entitled *Sume Pater Patrium.* He also made several recordings in Europe and the United States during this period.

In 1955, his Paris concerts demonstrated once again, his prestige in France. Here are a few press extracts:

"In truth, there are few composers able, without incurring great risks, to occupy an entire program. Once again, Heitor Villa-Lobos has thus been honored by the National Orchestra, and survived the challenge to his advantage." (René Dumesnil, *Le Monde*, 6-14-55.)

"A Villa-Lobos concert is always something to delight in: powerful, eruptive, with the constant characteristic that the listener is always breathless." (Marc Pincherle, *Nouvelles Litteraires*, 3-24-55.)

"Triumphant welcome from a justifiably enthusiastic public." (René Dumesnil, *Le Monde*, 3-22-55.)

"The name of Villa-Lobos shines to the most distant frontiers." Maurice Imbert, *L'Information*, 3-25-55.)

Still in 1955, the Richard Strauss Medal of the German Society for the Protection of Authors, Composers and Musicians was conferred upon him.

One must note here that Villa-Lobos always resided in Paris at 17, rue de l'Arcade, the Hotel Bedford, where the Emperor of Brazil, Pedro II, had resided towards the end of the 19th century.

In March 1957, he went to New York. During the last years of his life, this city was to be the center of his activities. His mother, to whom he was deeply attached, had died the preceding year in Rio. He felt then an unconquerable desire to travel about the world, to propagate his works and those of the principal Brazilian composers. On the occasion of his 70th birthday, he received numerous tributes, among which a Citation for Meritorious and Exceptional Services from the City of New York.

The New York Times published an editorial in his honor.[1]

1. *N.Y. Times*, 3-4-57 (Editorial)
"Heitor Villa-Lobos, Brazil's most famous composer and one of the truly distinguished men of music of our time, will be 70 tomorrow. His energy and enthusiasm are undiminished, and his creative powers remain at flood tide. He would be a remarkable figure in any age; in his own place and time he has been an enormously influential personality, leading his own people to a broadening of its culture and a rediscovery of its musical roots."

The Ministry of Education and Culture of Brazil instituted the Villa-Lobos Year, with a great program of celebrations. In September 1957, the city of São Paulo organized a Villa-Lobos week with readings, conferences and concerts.

In November of the same year, the composer visits Europe to record and to give concerts. The following year, he is in the United States and Europe once again, and he works on the film score of *Green Mansions* for Metro-Goldwyn-Mayer. In November he presents in Rio with the Brazilian Symphony Orchestra, the *Magnificat Alleluia.* Commissioned by the Vatican, the premiere of this choral work took place in Brazil by special permission of Pope Pius XII. On December 3, New York University conferred upon Villa-Lobos the title of Doctor Honoris Causa in Music. In the document given to the composer, we can read the following:

"Heitor Villa-Lobos, the eminent composer, is one of the most celebrated creative artists of our time. He has enriched the lives of several generations of students, and commands the musical destiny of a great number of future artists. A vibrant personality, endowed with the gift of communicating his enthusiasm, he has achieved world renown as a brilliant creator of modern music."

On this occasion, a choral work entitled *Bendita Sabedoria* (Blessed Wisdom) dedicated to the University of New York, was given its premiere performance.

In 1958, Villa-Lobos receives the Paris *Grand Prix du Disque* for his recording of the Suites from the *Discovery of Brazil.*

In January 1959, Villa-Lobos joins the Jury of the Pablo Casals International Competition in Mexico City, and travels immediately afterwards to Paris, London, Italy and Spain for concerts. In July he returns to Rio de Janeiro for the 50th Anniversary of Rio's opera house, (Teatro Municipal), and receives a commemorative medal for the city of his birth. Then his health gradually declined. He died November 17, 1959 in Rio de Janeiro. He was 72 years old.

4 / The Man

Before we examine the major works of Heitor Villa-Lobos, it would be well to portray, briefly, his controversial personality. To begin with, a personal recollection. I met him for the first time when I was only 17 years old. As a Sea Scout I had been assigned along with other teen-age Sea Scouts to help maintain order at a vacation colony near the St. John Fortress in Rio de Janeiro. The children of the colony were to sing at a festival for which Villa-Lobos came each morning to teach and prepare them. The young choristers were not always in the mood for singing and would not sit quietly and pay attention to the maestro. I was trying conscientiously to keep them in line, which was no easy job. At times Villa-Lobos would become so infuriated with their inattention and lack of discipline that he would distribute indiscriminate raps on the head. Although I am a tall man today, I was then not much taller than the other pupils, and in spite of my Scout uniform, the enraged composer dealt me one swift, hard knock on the head. For several years I smarted at the memory of this undeserved punishment, and not until I met Villa-Lobos under different circumstances and recounted the incident to him could I forgive him. He laughed so wholeheartedly about the whole affair that I had to relent.

Villa-Lobos was a musical genius: a genius by the prodigious richness of creation and the immeasurable musical talent which flowed from his pen. Like most geniuses, he had the defects of his qualities, and his behavior was not always exemplary. Rudeness wore the cloak of geniality, and his spontaneous exuberance was sometimes pure exhibitionism. His abhorrence of the mediocre and his compulsion *épater les bourgeois* contributed to his notoriety.

In 1913 he married Lucille Guimarães. She was a good pianist with an excellent musical background, whose influence on her husband is considered by many to have been remarkable. They had no children and separated in the late thirties. The composer then lived with Arminda de Almeida, a pupil considerably younger than himself, who became a devoted companion.

The Brazilian composer was a man of radiant charm. It was absolutely impossible to refuse him anything and he asked much! At first meeting he would seem shy, then would relax and enjoy the company. He would smile frequently between puffs of an enormous cigar, gesture like a Neapolitan, and choke on the cigar smoke, shaking as if in a frenzy. He would then sink into an armchair, smooth his disordered hair, and lapse into delighted guttural laughter.

But he was not really very fond of social life. He lived in downtown Rio in a small apartment, the walls of which were covered with photographic souvenirs. He composed with the radio going full blast, and simply loved corny radio dramas. He preferred to dress casually: single-breasted sack coats, checkered colored shirts, and queer ties. Almost to the last months of his life he maintained his lively, irascible disposition.

He was a conceited man. He was also rude, a character trait often discernible in his music—boyish rudeness it is true, but sometimes violent and shocking. He was a good friend to all those who cherished him, but he could also be a formidable enemy.

He was not a good performer, even of his own music. In his youth, he played the cello well but later he did not dare play in public. He played the piano with a certain superficial ease and was completely familiar with the mechanics of all instruments. As a conductor, he took certain liberties in the interpretation of scores, which the orchestra could not always understand at the first rehearsal. As a lecturer, he was— Villa-Lobos.

Was he a great musician in the full sense of the word? Yes. What charms us most is the purity, the vigor, and the personal character of his inspiration. His was not a mechanical skill but one of invention and vitality—completely without convention. Like most geniuses, he had his ups and downs. He was a "musical father" in that his latest child was always his favorite.

He was definitely self-taught. His stay in Europe in the twenties contributed greatly to the maturing of his style and to the cultural maturing of the man, but there it stopped. In Paris he acquired all the technical and aesthetic means of expression afforded by long contact with celebrated masters of contemporary art. Left to his own devices, he returned instinctively to revolutionary and undirected writing. Too often the self-taught musician emerges to cast a shadow over his works. Nevertheless, in Paris he had found his musical path and followed it as long as his strength permitted, to become the undisputed avant-gardist of Latin America.

He understood the orchestra well. Although not a truly accomplished pianist, he was an extraordinary composer of piano music. His knowledge of his favorite instrument, the cello, was remarkable. His fellow Brazilian composer, Toscanini's favorite, Francisco Mignone, defended him in these terms: "Villa-Lobos' musical form must be studied and evaluated in relation to Villa-Lobos himself. When he writes a fugue, we may laugh, but what we must do is to understand, analyze, enjoy, and repudiate or applaud the form that Villa-Lobos has given to *his* fugue and not compare it to any other fugue. Don't we proceed in this manner with the fugues of Frescobaldi or Mozart? Why not consider the fugues of Villa-Lobos from the same point of view? There are those who say that in Villa-Lobos' orchestrations one finds instrumental trifles which are ineffectual. Well, such faults are often encountered in the best works of the most renowned symphonists. We must not forget that a new seating arrangement for the orchestra or even the use of loud speakers could make such instrumental trifles sound very effective."[1]

1. Francisco Mignone, *A Parte do Anjo* (São Paulo, 1947), p. 53.

If Carlos Gomes was the best composer of the Americas in the nineteenth century, Heitor Villa-Lobos is considered by many as the greatest musical talent of his time in the Western Hemisphere.[2] Brazil is honored and proud to claim both these geniuses as native sons. To certify the enormous popularity of Villa-Lobos today, one need only glance at a recent record catalog. Very few contemporary composers have had so much of their music recorded for posterity as has Villa-Lobos. Through the medium of Italian opera, Carlos Gomes made several Brazilian tales such as "The Guarany" and "The Slave" popular in Europe. Villa-Lobos has presented to the world a series of characteristic Brazilian folk music, strange and unfamiliar to most music lovers. To non-Brazilians, his music may sound a little exotic, but to Brazilians this touch is an exact identification of their national music.

The position of Villa-Lobos in the history of Brazilian music is a fundamental one, for his works divide it into two periods. He was the creator of Brazilian national music and he is still the nation's best composer. He never began a "school" of his own, as he had little time for teaching, but his music has been the guide for every contemporary Brazilian composer, and in this sense his influence remains as strong as ever.

It would be extremely difficult to divide his works into clearly defined periods. The complexity of his temperament plus the contradictions of some of his compositions would confuse the reader. Therefore, a little arbitrarily perhaps, I prefer to examine his works by type rather than in chronological order. However, chronologically speaking, it should be said that after he became 60 years of age in 1947, there was a decline in the quality and quantity of his production. One reason for this was the natural tapering-off process in

2. On January 15, 1955, the *Philadelphia Evening Bulletin* said "it was a musically historical day for Philadelphia, for Villa-Lobos, whom many rate as the greatest composer to emerge from the relatively new Western Hemisphere, conducted a program of his own music." The well-known French art critic, Clarendon, who always opposed Villa-Lobos, recently conceded in writing: *Il a du genie, mais il n'a pas du talent"* (He has genius, but he has no talent).

a person of this age, even in one of Villa-Lobos' prodigious vitality. Another was that a serious disease with which he was afflicted had begun to trouble him. But he summoned up a great part of his tremendous energy and traveled extensively, conducting his works in places as far away as Israel and San Francisco.

His musical production, however, had suffered a blow. Frequent travel and hotel living were hardly conducive to the creation of masterpieces. His writings were only echoes of earlier triumphs. Expenses pertaining to his illness consumed a large part of his savings, which were partially restored by generous commissions from friends and cultural institutions. Villa-Lobos used what was left of his failing vitality to show the world what he had accomplished. From a rather egotistical musician he transformed himself into a champion of Brazilian music abroad, using his prestige to publicize other talented Brazilian composers and to make known some of his compositions which had not yet caught the attention of the music lovers of all latitudes. By such a final effort, Villa-Lobos is a credit to Brazil and to all Brazilians who are proud of the cultural achievements of their country.

*Reception at the Waldorf Astoria
in 1944*

5 / The Chôros

VILLA-LOBOS WAS FAMILIAR with all aspects of musical Brazil. His travels around the country, the permanent contact with *chorões,* his innate nationalism, all provided him with abundant material for the creation of music that was authentically Brazilian. Although he absorbed much in his youth, a large part of his national conscience was to be awakened by the aesthetic debates surrounding the "Week of Modern Art." He had experimented with national music in *Lenda do Caboclo* ("Legend of the Backwoodsman") and the *Canções Tipicas Brasileiras,* but it was not until 1922 that he chose it as a definitive means of musical expression. He then wrote *Noneto,* the *Chôros,* the *Serestas,* and the *Cirandas,* which are classed among his masterpieces.

When Villa-Lobos composed the *Chôro No. 1* in 1920, he was trying a new musical form in which he endeavored to portray in a strongly syncopated guitar solo the romantic aura of Rio's popular musicians. *Chôro No. 2,* written in Paris in 1924, is also nonambitious and does not reveal the significance that the *Chôros* series finally reached in his musical creation. It is a nostalgic duo for flute and clarinet with some typical Brazilian touches that charm the listener.

No doubt his sojourn in Europe was very propitious to the composition of the *Chôros* series. A better knowledge of the works of contemporary composers like Debussy, Stravinsky, and those who belonged to the "Group of Six" in Paris opened new horizons which until then had been unperceived by him. New technical skills, together with the longing for the distant homeland, evoked in Villa-Lobos powerful musical memories that were the basis for this monumental series of *Chôros,* so representative of Brazilian music. Although here and there one may notice the Impressionist influence, some coincidence with the rhythmic insistence of Stravinsky's *Rite of Spring*, or an inadequate or redundant theme, the complex of the *Chôros* is impressive. It represents the most valuable Brazilian contribution to contemporary music, being a true expression of national temperament in its many different aspects, and making appropriate use of Brazilian themes, musical cells, rhythms, and typical instruments.

The *Chôros* series itself is original. The component pieces were not written in consecutive order. Sometimes when Villa-Lobos was working on a certain piece, an idea for another would occur to him. He would build his work around that theme or rhythm and then give it a higher number in the series, in the expectation of eventually writing something in between. That is why it will be noticed that *Chôros No. 7, 8,* and *10* are dated 1924 and 1925, while *Chôros No. 4, 5,* and *6* were actually written in 1925. It should be noted also that the *Introduction to the Chôros* was composed in 1929. The series consists of a total of 16 pieces, ranging from guitar solo to the large canvas of *Chôro No. 13* for two orchestras and military band.

The *Introduction to the Chôros* (1929), for orchestra, was built in the traditional form of an overture by using motifs of all the *Chôros* except those numbered 1, 2, and 11. In the last bars, in a soft atmosphere, the author prepares for the beginning of *Chôro No. 1* by a guitar solo *cadenza ad libitum. Chôros No. 1* and *2* have already been mentioned. *Chôro No. 3* (1925), also known as *The Woodpecker,* was dedicated to the musical background of primitive Indians of the states of Mato Grosso and Goiás. It was written for clarinet, saxophone, bassoon, three horns, trombone, and male chorus *a cappella.* This *Chôro* has as its main theme the well-known Parcecis Indian song "Nozani-Na" and is particularly impressive through the daring flexibility in handling the male chorus. Villa-Lobos persists in the use of original onomatopoeic effects already experienced in the Fifth Symphony and *Noneto,* and later even more developed in *Chôros No. 10* and *14.*

Chôro No. 4 (1926), which used to be especially dear to the composer, was written for three horns and a trombone. It is very representative as *chôro* music and we are easily transported to suburban areas of Rio in the 1900's through the effective depiction of ironic lyricism expressed in mutes and gliding notes.

Chôro No. 5 (1926) for piano solo is a famous battle piece for virtuosi. It contains some curious rhythmic combinations not too distantly related to rubato which identify the serenaders' style. It is an essentially Brazilian piece, as expressed by its subtitle "Brazilian Soul."

The next *Chôro,* dated 1926, is of considerably larger scope than the preceding ones. A plaintive theme introduced by the flute (the typical instrument of Rio popular music) begins *Chôro No. 6,* which pulsates with persistent rhythms. Later in this piece, another memory of social life in the rural areas of Brazil is evoked by a little waltz on the bassoon.

Chôro No. 7, written in 1924 for a chamber music ensemble (flute, oboe, clarinet, saxophone, bassoon, violin, and cello), is also known as *Setemino.* It presents at the beginning a certain Amerindian touch; but later it offers some urban aspects of Rio, thanks to a vague melody, full of the appoggiature so frequent in the quick, gay polkas of the nineties. *Setemino* ends with a reminiscence of the first theme.

The *Dance Chôro,* or *Chôro No. 8,* composed in 1925, may be considered one of the strongest in the series. It is representative of Rio Carnival time with its multiple aspects and traditions. This work was solidly constructed by using an intricate counterpoint and requires, besides the full orchestra, two pianos, one employed as soloist and the other as a percussion instrument. *Chôro* No. 8 starts with an obstinate rhythm marked by the typical instrument *cara-caxá,* followed by a sensual theme of the popular *chôro* expressed by the bassoon, to which the trombone answers with another theme extracted from the initial one. At number 14 a rhythmic figure appears accompanied by a strange melody, with some very strong music that becomes more and more hallucinatory and barbaric.[1] This part ends with a plytonal chord

1. Orchestral scores are divided into numbered parts to facilitate rehearsals.

of the eleventh, of surprising effect. Of special note in this masterpiece is the slow, powerful, exotic march which begins at number 21, and a little later the sort of *batuque* (Negro dance) inspired by the popular composer Ernesto Nazaré, introduced by the first piano.

Chôro No. 9 for orchestra was written in 1929. It is a beautiful composition of really pure music. The author himself said of it, "There is no fiction, no memories, and no transfigured thematic factors, just rhythm and mechanical sounds." At number 23 one may notice a remarkable combination of Brazilian native instruments, used alternately in ¾ and ⅝ time. This work has seldom been played because of the difficulty in obtaining some of these typical instruments.

The next *chôro* in the series is considered by many musicologists to be one of Villa-Lobos' best contributions to modern music. It is a model of mastery and virtuosity in orchestration. In Brazil, *Chôro No. 10* is also known as *Rasga o Coração* ("Heartrending") because it appears to contain some traces of the popular song by that name written by Anacleto de Medeiros. In France it was presented as the ballet *Jurupary,* an Indian legend imagined by Vitorino de Carvalho and first interpreted by the famous Serge Lifar.

The beginning of *Chôro No. 10* depicts the groves and the Brazilian forests. What a prodigious variety of birds is revealed to us by the flutes and clarinets! At the second measure of letter F, the first fragment of the main theme appears: a pentatonic melody. At number 5, in the low register of the bassoon, the composer introduces a bizarre and obstinate theme which influences all elements in the orchestra, especially the complex choral polyphony. The text sung by the mixed chorus has no literary sense, giving the author the opportunity to obtain curious onomatopoeic effects. When the voices reach a climactic crescendo, there emerges in a secondary plan, hardly identifiable through the intricate counterpoint, a sentimental melody—"Heartrending." The *Chôro,* one of Heitor Villa-Lobos' most perfect realizations, ends in a grandiose fortissimo by both chorus and orchestra.

Chôro No. 11 (1928), for piano and orchestra, is the longest in the series. The technique is the same as in the preceding *Chôros* but the intentions are different. It is definitely a much more subjective work, without express concern for reproducing musical elements of Brazilian nature. A heavy and imposing piece, it is also a challenge to the piano virtuoso who ventures to perform its extensive and difficult cadenza.

Chôro No. 12 was composed in 1929 for a large orchestra, the author's intention being to improve certain techniques tried out in *Chôro No. 9*. One perceives a remarkable artistic maturity and an unusual balance in the construction of this work. "It is strong, and as big and robust as an old elephant," Villa-Lobos said of it in 1947. At number 34 there is a sequence of dissonant chords with two systematic modulations; at number 85, the oboes interpret a theme which reminds one of the old Brazilian dance called *esquinado,* collected by the author in the state of Espirito Santo. Finally, at number 91, the listener runs into an unexpected rhythmical disarticulation of queer effects.

Chôro No. 13, also written in 1929, for two orchestras and military band, has its principal theme vertically harmonized in free canon. This work, which at the start presents a classical aspect, is suddenly assailed by an orgy of sounds, rhythms, and tone colors at the military band's attack point. There, the two orchestras become mere accompanists of the military band, the first taking over the high scale and the second performing the low notes. Once these agitated and colorful measures are ended, a new atmosphere of percussion sounds begins with the assistance of native Brazilian instruments. Surprisingly, *Chôro No. 13* ends in a pianissimo by the string quintets of the two orchestras.

Chôro No. 14, composed earlier in 1928, is also difficult to perform. Written for orchestra, military band, and chorus, it is perhaps the most monumental and the most violent of them all. It may be considered a synthesis of all the aesthetic elements of the series. Its harmonic and thematic complexity is prodigious, giving the impression of its having been built with enormous sound blocks. Villa-Lobos here tried writing music for chorus in quarter notes, stressing in the score an intentional dissonance with special symbols. It ends with a canonic rondo, in which each player stops playing, one after the other. The last one is the violin *spala* which rests on two prolonged notes, in double strings, at an interval of a minor second. They keep fading out until they vanish.

Two Chôros Bis (1928), for violin and cello, were not written as a part of the series. Villa-Lobos composed a duo in two parts and, as this work was conceived instinctively in the manner of the *Chôros*, he gave it that title. It is a remarkable example of the master's skillfulness in handling the strings. He was so resourceful in the use of these two instruments that the duo often seems to be a string quartet.

As a whole, the *Chôros* series is extremely important within the canon of Villa-Lobos' work, by both its aesthetic and formal construction.

6 / The Brazilian Bachianas

THE SERIES OF NINE *Brazilian Bachianas* is a complex of works inspired by the musical atmosphere of Bach's style, which Villa-Lobos considered a source of universal folklore and a link uniting all peoples. Although the *Brazilian Bachianas* constitute an aesthetic retrogression for a composer who wrote the *Chôros,* they represent a valuable experiment in the juxtaposition of certain harmonic counterpoints and the melodic atmosphere of rural or urban areas of Brazil to the music of Johann Sebastian Bach.

The *Brazilian Bachiana No. 1* (1930) for eight cellos was written for the symphony concerts conducted by Burle Marx in Rio de Janeiro. The first part, an *embolada,* is a quick folk song of onomatopoeic effect. Villa-Lobos obtained from the very beginning a simultaneous atmosphere typically Brazilian and harmoniously classic. At the seventh measure, a long and low melody appears that spiritualizes some of Bach's techniques without losing the initial rhythm. The second part of the Bachiana, a romantic *modinha,* starts languidly and huskily. Its main theme, constructed in the form of a Bach aria, begins with a long and plaintive melody, followed by a *più mosso.* This movement ends very effectively with a melody played pianissimo by solo cello. The fugue, Villa-Lobos said, was composed in the style of Satiro Bilhar, an old *chorão* and friend of Villa-Lobos. The fugue represents a conversation between four *chorões,* each one striving to obtain thematic primacy in successive questions and answers with a dynamic crescendo.

The *Bachiana No. 2* for chamber orchestra was also written in 1930 and is probably the most popular of the series. In the first part, the prelude, the composer depicts an old Rio type, the *capadocio* (a sort of rogue), who comes to us swaggering sinuously in the adagio. The aria possesses the musical atmosphere of fetichist *macumbas* and *candomblés,* while the third movement is a dance entitled, "Souvenir of the Backlands." Both stray somewhat from Bach's climate in spite of the progression of modulant basses to be found in the dance. The final toccata, better known as "The Little Train," is a charming piece of descriptive impressions evoked by travels in the old trains of the interior of Brazil. Villa-Lobos did not wish merely to describe a locomotive in action, as Honneger successfully did in *Pacific 231;* he wanted to create the atmosphere of old rural Brazil by superimposing on it a delicate folk melody.

Bachiana No. 3 for piano and orchestra begins with a long adagio phrase almost in the form of a recitative, and played by the solo instrument. Another melody in the low register played by the orchestra is heard in counterpoint with the piano. This produces, perhaps, an atmosphere too similar to Bach. The structure of the second movement, "Fantasy," although presented in the form of a musical reverie, has the character of an aria. The *più mosso* introduces a second episode, gay and lively, upon which the pianist may exhibit his virtuosity. This aria has a beautiful Brazilian theme with simple counterpoint, while the toccata tries to reproduce folk dances from Northeast Brazil without getting too far away from the Bachian style.

The next Bachiana was composed in 1930, originally for piano solo and later fully orchestrated (1936). Especially to be noted are the second movement chorale, serene and almost religious, and the lively *miudinho,* a folk dance. The dance character is revealed by the melodic design of sixteenth notes, irregularly rhythmic. An incisive and vibrant melody of obvious popular savor emerges on the trombone at number 1 in the score. An insistent, very low pedal point, like the sound of a large organ, is reminiscent of Bach in this dance.

The *Bachiana No. 5* for soprano and eight cellos is also

very well known to the American public thanks to a famous recording by Bidu Sayão. It has two parts only: an aria ("Cantilena") written in 1938 and a dance ("Martelo") dated 1945. The first is undoubtedly one of Villa-Lobos' master-pieces. Its introduction of a 2/5 time in pizzicato well defines the atmosphere of Rio guitar serenaders at the turn of the century. Then the author produces a languid lyric melody gliding on pizzicati in counterpoint, whose polyphony is sup-ported by a slow march of cadenced basses in the manner of Bach. At number 7 another melody in a quicker tempo emerges in the style of the old *modinha* (a sentimental song), only to return later to the initial thematic situation, as a re-exposition. The second part, the dance, brings an obstinate rhythm characteristic of the *desafio* (musical challenge) so typical of the Northeast of Brazil. Villa-Lobos said that he tried to create its main theme from fragments of bird songs of that region.

The only Brazilian Bachiana which is truly chamber music is the sixth, for flute and bassoon. This work begins with a sorrowful modulation for the flute, but almost immediately, in the second measure, the bassoon takes up a Brazilian theme in an admirable fusion of the *chôro* with Bach's style. This duo shows considerable inventiveness and the second movement is even more attractive in form and ideas. The allegro possesses a remarkable vigor within the limited musi-cal range of a duo.

The *Bachiana No. 7*, written for orchestra in 1942, is di-vided into four parts: prelude, *gigue,* toccata, and fugue, the latter two being the most interesting movements. The toccata, which is especially attractive, has a main theme emerging from festive tones, quick rhythms, and dissonant harmonies, like an evocation of the folk singer who challenges his con-tender. The musical construction of this movement is truly magnificent not only for its technical value but for its de-scriptive qualities as well.

In the *Brazilian Bachiana No. 8,* also for orchestra, the third movement, a toccata, should be emphasized. The initial theme, scherzando, is played by the oboes in the manner of the *catira batida*, a dance and song from Central Brazil. The first exposition is rather more rhythmic than melodic. A coda of four measures, prestissimo, surprisingly ends the toccata.

Finally, the last piece of the series, the *Bachiana No. 9*, was written for chorus *a cappella*, or "voice orchestra." This Bachiana, difficult to perform, represents for many critics the climax of Villa-Lobos' compositions for voice. Some original and very personal effects experimented with in the *Symphony No. 5* and perfected in *Noneto, Chôro No. 10*, and *Mandú Sararâ*, have reach an unusual degree of virtuosity. The prelude in slow tempo, rather mysterious, is entrusted to six mixed voices. At number 91, the harmonic atmosphere becomes polytonal until the fermata, which ends this part. The fugue for six voices is ably developed until the emergence, majestic and dominating, of a melody in three octaves in the form of a chorale. Other episodes follow with new rhythmic, harmonic, and contrapuntal dispositions, but always maintaining thematic unity. The final cadenza is sung by all performers on the vowel "o." This work is indeed rich in tone colors obtained by means of surprising onomatopoeic effects with syllables and vowels.

Reception in honour of Villa-Lobos at the residence of Consul Dora Vasconcellos in New York in 1957

7 / Ballets and Symphonic Poems

VILLA-LOBOS' FIRST EXPERIMENT in this field seems to date from 1910, in the *Suite de Cantos Sertanejos* ("Suite of Backwoodsmen's Songs"). After a series of less important works, he produced two significant symphonic poems in 1917: *Uirapurú* and *Amazon,* the latter being a revision of *Miremis.* Although usually associated, these pieces are far apart aesthetically as well as formally. *Uirapurú* is all poetry, a naive story of the Brazilian forests; *Amazon* is possessed by a savage spirit, vibrating with cosmic force. As Mário de Andrade describes it: "The orchestra moves forward painfully, dragging itself, breaking branches, felling trees, and tonalities, and treatises on composition." [1]

Based on a story written by Villa-Lobos himself, *Uirapurú* is a delicate Amerindian panel in which the author has experimented with new tone colors, introducing some typical Brazilian instruments and using percussion with restraint.

Amazon, embodying the composer's chaotic impressions of a trip to that region, stands in towering contrast to its companion piece. It contains remarkable orchestral effects and daring combinations of tone colors as well as the use of violinophone and *viola d'amore* as solo instruments. All this is developed with deliberate tonal freedom. "After 'Amazon,'" Villa-Lobos said, "I lost all prudence and shyness about writing daring things."

The four suites, *Discovery of Brazil,* were composed in 1937 for a moving picture of the same name. They were

1. *Música, Doce Música* (São Paulo, 1932).

inspired by the main episodes of Cabral's voyage of discovery, described in the famous letter written by Pero Vaz de Caminha to King Manuel of Portugal: the departure from Portugal, a Moorish impression, a sentimental adagio expressing the feeling of solitude at sea, and then, successively, the discovery scene, the procession of the Cross, and the first Mass in Brazil. For this finale an important *a cappella* choral piece was composed, consisting of a Gregorian kyrie for male chorus and an Amerindian melody, with a Tupi-Guaraní text, for female chorus, sung simultaneously. The result is truly grandiose.

Extracted from an amazon legend collected by folklorist Barbosa Rodrigues, the ballet *Mandú Sarará* (1940) contains some of the best music written by Villa-Lobos. The author achieved excellent results by combining a children's chorus with an adult chorus for expressing the fear of two children captured by the forest devil, Curupira; also effective is the use of descending glissandi. Mandú Sarará, the spirit of the dance, helps the children to fool the monster and rejoin their parents in safety as they once more sing and play. This piece has an impressive and attractive sonority, especially when the main theme passes from the baritones and basses to the whole imposing choral mass.

Recent symphonic works confirm Villa-Lobos' mastery of the orchestra, but they have left his admirers disappointed. This is the period in which the composer traveled too often and his work seems to reflect this lack of stability. Most of these works, furthermore, are a result of commissions, which may have dulled the composer's spontaneity. He was now beginning to rest upon the many laurels obtained by so many years of arduous effort. Old themes and whole movements of earlier little-known works were recast for commercial purposes. *Erosion* (1950), commissioned by the Louisville Orchestra, is a cocktail of several previous Amerindian symphonic poems, starting with *Amazon* (which was already a recast of *Miremis).* The ballet *Ruda, God of Love* (1951), was commissioned by the La Scala Opera House of Milan and was a disappointment in Paris in 1954. Divided into three long parts, it contains nothing new. I have never heard *The Odyssey of a Race,* dedicated to (and the copyright donated to) the State of Israel, in 1953; but the consensus was not one of praise.

The ballet *Emperor Jones,* for orchestra with baritone and contralto solos, is an exception within this period. It was commissioned for the Ellenville Festival and performed there with José Limon as the soloist. Eugene O'Neill's story presented a challenge to the composer and this work meets it effectively; it is a high mark in this period of "practical" production.

Finally, the music for the motion picture *Green Mansions,* although not daring, was spontaneously delicate and reminiscent of the *Uirapurú* days. But he was no longer an innovator.

8 / Concertos and Symphonies

A CHECK OF A CATALOG of Villa-Lobos' works will reveal a long list of both concertos and symphonies. None of them, however, has really attained success either in Brazil or even abroad, although they carry special weight among the composer's works. The large majority of concertos was composed after his success in the United States in 1945. Almost all were commissioned by artists and foreign cultural organizations.

An old work which is still attractive is the *Fantasy of Mixed Movements* (1922), a series of three pieces called, respectively, "Convulsive Soul," "Serenity," and "Contents," written for violin and orchestra or violin and piano. It was composed in a very original and personal manner, demanding considerable skill from the soloist. The work contains some of the best music for violin ever written in Brazil.

The *Concerto No. 1* for piano and orchestra (1945), in four movements, was commissioned, first performed, and recorded by the Canadian pianist Ellen Ballon. The Cadenza and the andante are representative of Villa-Lobos' skillful handling of the piano. *The Concerto No. 2,* written in 1948 and first played by Souza Lima in 1950, has a lovely lento movement but little else which is novel.

The *Concerto for Harp and Orchestra* (1953), dedicated to Nicanor Zabaleta and first performed by him, was better received by the public. The *Philadelphia Evening Bulletin* (January 15, 1955) praised the beautiful andante and the captivating scherzo as well as the long and very difficult cadenza.

The 1951 *Concerto for Guitar,* especially written for Andrés Segovia, is scored for small orchestra. The solo instrument is subdued, except for a point or two of moderate stress, until it is given, between the second and final movements, an extended solo cadenza which deals richly in ornamentation and transmutation of the principal themes.

The *Concerto No. 4* for piano and orchestra was played first by the Brazilian pianist Bernard Segall in Pittsburgh. Comments from the press were not favorable. The *Post-Gazette* (January 18, 1953), after comparing it to German romantics and Tschaikowsky, stated that "the opening movement utilizes the piano ornamentally rather than principally and the scherzo as well as the final movement is unresolved. There is an excellent and well-written cadenza for the solo piano, but generally the instrument is too often subordinate to the orchestration."

The *Concerto No. 5* for piano and orchestra, dedicated to Felicia Blumenthal and first performed by the London Philharmonic Orchestra conducted by Jean Martinon, drew negative comments from the *Times* (May 10, 1955). "Villa-Lobos is the Telemann of our times. The new concerto is emotionally high-powered, full of surging tones and noisy climaxes. They are not unpleasant to listen to, but they cut little ice. Some of the quiet passages, as for instance the piano's first entrance, make a more than theatrical effect. The piano part is a telling, even a fulsome one. From the heart the whole concerto doubtless comes; on the heart its effect is momentary, not lasting."

In the same year, we have the *Concerto No. 2 for Cello and Orchestra,* commissioned by Aldo Parisot and first performed by this noted Brazilian cellist and the New York Philharmonic Orchestra. The work is conceived in four movements, although the last two may be considered as one, and the author has given it a slight Brazilian folkloric touch. A wave of lyricism submerges the listener, especially in the characteristic andante.

The *Concerto for Harmonica,* commissioned by John Sebastian, does not seem to have been presented to the public as yet. I know only that it was composed in 1954.

Villa-Lobos has written twelve symphonies. The first was

conceived in a classical form and the last two movements are of some interest. The *Symphony No. 2* (The Ascension), written in 1917, requires a large orchestra and several typically Brazilian instruments. Its thematic treatment is quite original and the work contains fluent rhythms and attractive harmonies. Composed in the cyclical form suggested by d'Indy, it has a beautiful main theme and a romantic andante moderato. The allegro offers a mysterious clarinet solo accompanied by a tamtam which leads the symphony to a dramatic finale.

Symphonies No. 3, 4, and *5* are of less importance and were intended to depict the author's impressions of war, victory, and peace, respectively. I might stress that in the Fifth Symphony (1920) he used onomatopoeic texts for chorus, a device which he was to develop later in *Noneto* and the *Chôro No. 10,* and which was highly successful.

The *Symphony No. 6,* written twenty-four years later, was constructed in quite a contrasting style. The first five were exuberant and classical in form, while the other six, dating from 1944 to 1956, are clearly affiliated with the new personal style which Villa-Lobos perfected in forty years of prodigious effort to express the Brazilian soul. This later technique, which had been materializing since 1938, especially in the chamber music, is a concentrated musical language: synthetic, less nationalistic, and more in accord with modern industrialized Brazil. The source for the main theme of the Sixth Symphony was a mountain skyline near Rio, interpreted by using a personal method called "milimeterization" (based on the use of a graph).

The Seventh Symphony, of which Villa-Lobos was very fond, also requires a large orchestra and skillful handling. A more diluted Brazilian feeling, almost imperceptible within the dense orchestral texture, pervades this subjective work which illustrates so well the author's dynamic talent. The main theme, played by the bassoon, was built with the letters of the word *America,* using "A" as the first one. The scherzo is very original and expresses the tragic dilemma of mankind oscillating between peace and war.

The *Symphony No. 8,* written in 1950, was well received in Philadelphia five years later. The *Inquirer* praised the slow movement, always Villa-Lobos' forte, and the rich rhythmical variety, but found it "too romantic." The Ninth Symphony seems to have been composed in 1951 but has never been performed, and I have no data on it.

The composer wrote his *Symphony No. 10* in 1952. Some suspect that it is, in fact, the Ninth, revised at the moment he received a commission to compose a special work to commemorate the São Paulo Quadricentennial. It was conceived for soloists, chorus, and orchestra, and was based on the poem "Beata Vergine" by Father José de Anchieta, a pioneer Portuguese priest of the sixteenth century. It was first performed in Paris on April 4, 1957, by the Radio Symphony Orchestra and the French Television Chorus. Clarendon, an acid art critic (*Le Figaro,* April 6-7, 1957), is perhaps too severe in his judgment: "The symphony on the whole expressed fatigue and distilled formidable boredom."

The Eleventh Symphony was commissioned by the Boston Symphony Orchestra and first performed there on March 2, 1956, conducted by the composer. It had been composed two years earlier at the request of the Koussevitsky Foundation. This large and busy score is essentially a late romantic expression with a contemporary manner. The normally conservative Boston audience buzzed with approval and the *Boston Globe* applauded it as "among the very best of the 75th Anniversary commissioned music we have heard so far." The *Boston Herald,* however, stressed that "the profusion of material is so concentrated, with one idea tumbling after another, the listener is more than likely to get lost in the bewildering profusion of the musical thought." In fact, many of Villa-Lobos' late works show a tendency to prolixity and overcrowding of musical ideas. This emphasis on complexity could well be an attempt to conceal his difficulty in keeping up with the musicalaesthetic evolution of the twentieth century. In any event, the *Christian Science Monitor* the following day aptly described the atmosphere: "A new Symphony by Heitor Villa-Lobos is a world event."

The *Symphony No. 12* was a hit at the first Inter-American Music Festival in Washington in April, 1958. It expressed all the orchestral resources and rich romantic textures the Brazilian composer could master in his long artistic career. In this initial hearing, it proved a smasher even if some would label it old-fashioned. The severe Washington critic Paul Hume remarked: "The first movement has a big build-up not unlike that of a fine Broadway musical, only this is the kind of work from which Broadway learns its lessons. It had all the kind of wide-screen, multilux color effect I thoroughly enjoyed. Its pulse, its juicy progressions, its stem-winding textures may be on the way out, but if they are, symphony concerts are going to be duller for it" (*Washington Post,* April 21, 1958). The use of brass instruments in this symphony is particularly effective.

Most of Villa-Lobos' symphonies, especially those written in the last few years of his life, are difficult to perform. Unfortunately, many conductors hesitate to play orchestral works which require several rehearsals and therefore tax their budgets, alas too frequently strained. It is sincerely hoped that this hurdle may be overcome in view of obtaining more performances of Villa-Lobos' orchestral masterpieces.

There were also two *sinfonietas* which deserve to be mentioned, the second of which was dedicated to the Roman Academy of Music and first performed there. It is a charming piece quite representative of the most refined, mature Villa-Lobos.

*Rehearsal with singer Phyllis Curtis in
New York, December, 1958*

9 / Chamber Music

THE CATALOG OF CHAMBER MUSIC by Villa-Lobos is one of the largest and most effective in the entire Latin American repertoire. Being himself a master of the cello and a qualified performer of chamber music, as a composer he succeeded in producing several masterpieces of lasting popularity in this aesthetically difficult medium.

In his youth he wrote seven sonatas, among which special value should be attached to the *Sonata No. 2* (1916), for cello and piano, a work of solid structure without folklore influences. He also composed five trios, of which the First Trio (1911) anticipates, in the final allegro, his later experimentation with the blending of Bach's style and Brazilian musical elements in the *Bachianas Brasileiras*. The *Trio No. 3* for oboe, clarinet, and bassoon is often performed and proves fascinating in its rhythmical audacity and its exciting challenge to the virtuosity of the performers. The last trio, dating from 1945, is free from any national influence. *Duo 1946* for violin and cello is an attractive piece with little national accent.

It is in his string quartets that Villa-Lobos made his best and most important contribution to contemporary chamber music. He wrote a total of seventeen string quartets in various styles, ranging from direct nationalism through what might be called "a transfigured folklorism," finally reaching a more universal type of expression. Arnaldo Estrella, in his study, *Brazilian Chamber Music*, stresses the significance of the Third Quartet (1916), also known as "The Popcorn Quartet" because the second movement employs the device of pizzicato with unusual insistence. The Fourth Quartet also has a second movement that is very popular, a technically difficult scherzo full of authentic Brazilian flavor.

The obvious musical nationalism of the Fifth Quartet appears to be quite spontaneous, in contrast to the deliberate concentration of Brazilian feeling achieved in its three successors. Although the Sixth Quartet, rich in ideas and imbued with an attractive *chorão* lyricism, is often played, the Seventh is the more extraordinary work. It unleashes a veritable tornado of ideas, in apparent disorder yet skillfully controlled and interwoven in the complex texture. The Seventh Quartet is virtually a nonthematic composition, with some Brazilian touches in the second movement, and admirable polyrhythmic effects in the other movements.

The Eighth and Ninth Quartets are works of excellent structure. The first movement of the former is remarkable for its rhythmic variety and its ingenious harmonic combinations. Particularly to be remarked is the beautiful, plaintive melody introduced by the first violin. The last movement is based on two contrasting themes: the one, powerful and dramatic; the other, carefree and gracious. The Ninth Quartet leaves musical nationalism behind in its search for universal expression. The first movement is an apotheosis of rhythm, inexhaustibly inventive, and revealing an amazing skill in writing for the instruments.

During the last ten years of his life, Villa-Lobos composed eight more quartets, all of them well written but with a tendency toward excessive complexity that may have hindered their effectiveness. As in so much of the music of Villa-Lobos, vivid and varied rhythmic patterns are the distinguishing feature of these quartets.

Concerning the Fifteenth Quartet, a critic of the *New York Times* (April 20, 1958) wrote, "The style is a compound of many influences and yet it manages to be individual." This is an observation that would be applicable to a great deal of Villa-Lobos' music. The lively scherzo of this quartet must be one of the shortest in musical history, running only a little over a minute.

The Brazilian critic Eurico Nogueira França bestows special praise upon the Sixteenth Quartet, which, together with its melodic fluency and inventive fertility, once again reveals the rhythmic wealth that was the composer's great achievement.

Among several pieces for violin may be mentioned *O Martirio dos Insetos* ("The Insects' Martyrdom") dating from 1925. It contains the celebrated virtuoso piece *Mariposa na Luz* ("A Moth in the Light"), which is highly descriptive but rather monotonous in spite of its frequent modulations. The final prestissimo is always effective on the concert stage. Another well-known piece is *The Song of the Black Swan* for violin on the fourth string or for cello with piano.

Villa-Lobos wrote many compositions for various instrumental combinations. Among the earliest of them is the *Quatuor* for harp, celesta, flute, saxaphone, and women's chorus, evoking impressions of urban life in Rio de Janeiro (where it was written in 1921). This composition reveals the passing influence of Debussy. The *Noneto* for chamber orchestra and chorus of mixed voices, composed in Paris in 1923, is remarkable above all for its attempt to convey a vivid musical impression of Brazil, from popular urban melodies (such as the tango by Nazareth called *Turuna)* to the animal sounds of the jungle and the primitive Amerindian and Afro-Brazilian chants. It is indeed a musical synthesis of Brazil in miniature. It reveals great harmonic freedom and rare instrumental ability; it is written for eight soloists and a battery of percussion instruments, in addition to the chorus of mixed voices which is treated as an independent instrument.

Several recent minor works might be mentioned, but they are not significant in the whole complex of Villa-Lobos' production. The most attractive of these are probably the *Duo* for oboe and bassoon (1957), the curious *Fantasy* for saxophone and piano, and the lovely *Concerto Grosso* commissioned by the American Wind Symphony.

10 / Piano Composition

ALTHOUGH VILLA-LOBOS was not a pianist and even less of a virtuoso, his piano works are first-rate and some of the most popular in contemporary musical literature. Here, too, it should be emphasized that rhythm is the main reason for his success. After the *African Dances* his concern with rhythm was increasingly accentuated in all his works. Always original and trying to avoid the routine at any price, his piano music bears the imprint of nationalism beginning with *The Baby's Family (Suite No. 1)* of 1918.

The first important piano compositions were the *African Dances,* written in 1914 and later orchestrated. They are divided into three parts: "Farrapos," "Kankikís," and "Kankukús."

Villa-Lobos' fondness for children is clearly reflected in his piano music. The three suites, *The Baby's Family* (1918, 1921, and 1926), the *Cirandas, The Carnival of Brazilian Children, Momo Precoce* ("Precocious Momus"), *Youthful Souvenirs, Historias da Carochinha* ("The Brazilian Mother Goose"), *Francette et Pia,* were all composed especially for children or as a result of the observation of children.

The Baby's Family suites, the first of which Artur Rubinstein has played so often, are based on Brazilian children's themes. The first series depicts dolls with contradictory temperaments; the second, children's pets; and the third, children's games. The dolls suite is indeed enchanting, and pianists confirm that the public finds it so. "The China Doll" is sweet and tender and very different from "Boneca de Massa" ("Clay Doll"), which is insinuating and decided. The clay doll interprets an Indian dance accompanied by the rhythm of the tamtam, while the rubber doll is all elasticity.

The black doll, a sort of wooden puppet, is particularly effective and leaves us with an impression of painful emptiness. Rhythm! Rhythm! "Punchinello" seems a noisy fellow whose only pleasure is to hammer our heads repreatedly with dry sticks, until it appears that the keeper of the children's shop goes mad with the continuous rapping and finally crushed Punchinello—or so the last measure suggests. The eighth doll is the witch and we can easily visualize her riding on a broom and frightening children.

In contrast to *The Baby's Family (Suite No. 1),* which is considerably influenced by Debussy, the Second Suite is dissonant, atonal, and polytonal. Dedicated to and first performed by Aline van Barentzen, it contains some remarkable *trouvailles,* although it never attained the popularity of the Frist Suite. The Third Suite is very little known and was never published.

One of the most applauded piano compositions by Villa-Lobos is *Lenda do Caboclo* ("The Legend of the Backwoodsman"), written in 1920 in nationalist style. A beautiful melancholic theme expresses a feeling of deep sorrow interrupted by an expansive *più mosso.* At the end, the mysterious aura returns, leaving a sensation of emptiness and isolation. There is also a good transcription for violin made by Pery Machado, which is very often played. The *Carnival of the Brazilian Children,* also written in 1920, contains the lively and popular "Little Pierrot's Jennet."

The *Rude Poema,* which was begun one year later for Artur Rubinstein and finished in 1926, is one of the most complex pieces of contemporary piano literature. The work begins with a bass melody in the left hand, answered by another melody in the right hand, both of which may be considered the main themes, reminiscences of which appear clearly in the rest of the composition. The climax in maddening fortissimo is obtained in the last five measures by means of four blows by the right hand on three low notes (C, B, and A). to complete this sonorous grandeur, Villa-Lobos used a permanent pedal, which contributes much to the creation of a savage and brutal atmosphere for this *Rude Poema.*

Many consider the series of sixteen *Cirandas* to be his piano masterpieces. They are pianistic, extremely rich in tone color and spontaneously-Brazilian, and actually deserve more attention than can be devoted to them here. In spite of the virtuosity of such pieces as "Fui no Tororó" ("I Went to Tororó") and "Olha o Passarinho, Domine" ("Look at the Bird, Domine"), the author has used children's themes with an admirable combination of simplicity and daring dissonance, all enveloped in a delicate atmosphere. The musical treatment given to such themes is always original, with great harmonic and rhythmic wealth. Sometimes they are slightly changed, as in "Therezinha de Jesus"; sometimes reproduced in all their simplicity, as in "Xo, Xo, Passarinho" ("Shoo, Shoo, Little Bird"); and sometimes considerably altered, as in "A Procura de uma Agulha" ("Looking for a Needle"). Some of the themes, such as "Que Lindos Olhos!" ("What Beautiful Eyes"), are not well known. Others like "O Pintor de Canay" ("The Painter of Canay") are quite banal, and at least one, "Vâmos Atrás da Serra, Calunga" ("Let's Go Beyond the Hills, Calunga"), presents symphonic characteristics. I am especially fond of "O Cravo Brigou com a Rosa" ("The Carnation Quarrelled with the Rose"), in which, on an original interpolated rhythm, the composer introduces a gay theme in different tonalities. "Nesta Rua, Nesta Rua" ("In This Street, in This Street") is certainly one of the best of this series, with a very effective cantabile section.

Momo Precoce, written in 1929 for piano and orchestra and commissioned by Magdalena Tagliaferro, is a brilliant and lively score using some of the themes from the series on the children's carnival. The piano has great responsibility and offers unexpected and amusing sounds. The collection of folksongs and piano music based on folk themes, *Practical Guide,* contains two real jewels: "A Maré Encheu" ("The Tide Came In") and "Na Corda da Viola" ("On the Strings of the Guitar"). Both are very simple but contain a harmonic texture of great richness.

Dated 1936, the well-known *Brazilian Cycle,* consisting of

four pieces in a rather ambitious style, is among Villa-Lobos' most popular works. The various pieces depict the backwoodsman who seeds his land, sings a serenade to the moon, then gives a "hillbilly" party and invites the "White Indian" to it. Effective results are obtained in "O Plantio do Caboclo" ("The Caboclo's Planting") through a rhythmic design expressing the regular clang of the plowshare. In "Impressões Seresteiras" ("Impressions of the Hinterland"), the hinterland atmosphere is evoked with all its sorrowfulness, and in "Festa no Sertão" ("Backwoods Party") the author truly achieved one of his best descriptive works, so varied are the musical devices used. Finally, "Dança do Indio Branco" ("Dance of the White Indian") portrays sensualism in a binary rhythm, developing a theme of great melodic and rhythmic beauty. This piece ends with an ascending modulation, accelerated and very brilliant.[1]

In the last twenty years of his production, Villa-Lobos was encouraged to write more music for the piano. He composed the valuable *As Tres Marias* ("The Three Marys"), *Saudades das Selvas Brasileiras* ("Longing for the Brazilian Jungle"), and *Homage to Chopin* written for the centennial of the Polish composer. But except for these, the concertos for piano and orchestra he wrote during this time were, unfortunately, not successful, whatever the reason for it might be.

1. Pianist Vieira Brandão, for a while a sort of official performer of Villa-Lobos' music, once said that he believed "The Dance of the White Indian" to be a kind of musical self-portrait of the composer.

Interval during rehearsal of a concert with the Philadelphia Orchestra January 15, 1955. Among others: Villa-Lobos, Andres Segovia, Nicanor Zabaleta, harpist Salgado, Walter Burle Marx, pianist Bernard Segal, Maestro Arthur Cohn

11 / Vocal Music

VILLA-LOBOS' songs, although not his greatest contribution to Brazilian music, have had a decided influence in the shaping and development of the *lied* (art song) in that country. The utilization of popular themes in classical music dates from 1869 in Brazil, as shown by Itiberê da Cunha's *Sertaneja,* but all previous attempts before Villa-Lobos were incipient. The only valuable work previous to his was that of Nepomuceno, but this was in regard to melody only. Few had harmonized folk songs, using folk themes or motifs, before 1919, the date of the *Brazilian Typical Songs.* Villa-Lobos had experimented with national song before with "Noite de Luar" ("Moonlight Evening") in 1912, and to some extent in "Sertão no Estio" ("Summer in the Back-woods"). Nevertheless, while these two songs had some typi-cal traits, they fell short of expressing the national character of Brazilian song.

The vocal works of Villa-Lobos may be divided into three periods: universal, directly folkloric, and indirectly folkloric, that is, utilizing advanced methods of handling the folklore. But these periods very often mingle.

Villa-Lobos is not the ideal composer for voice; most of his songs have become popular due to his touch of genius, not because of any special skill in handling vocal problems. His melodic line is frequently tortured, using intervals often considered dangerous for vocalists and creating singing problems that are difficult to solve.

"Confidence," the first song in his catalog, reveals a canta-bile style quite within the traditions of the epoch. "Mal Secreto" ("Secret Evil"), written in 1913, already demon-strates the composer's unusual gifts. A surprising melodic line is used to interpret the famous poem, enhanced by the continuous use of abrupt modulation. Another powerful rendition is the song called "Louco" ("The Madman") for baritone and orchestra, which is extremely dissonant and rather uncomfortable to perform.

Among his earlier works, the series *Miniatures* (1912-1917) is quite popular and offers two interesting songs: "Viola" ("Guitar") in which one notices some national traits, and especially, "Sino da Aldeia" ("The Village Bell"), audaciously dissonant. The author wanted to portray alternately the peeling of bells and heartbeats; in this respect the orchestral version is particularly interesting.

There are thirteen compositions in the series of *Brazilian Typical Songs* (1919) covering almost every folkloric field. The last three were composed and incorporated in the series as late as 1935. The themes are not original with Villa-Lobos but are harmonizations of familiar folk motifs. "Ena Makocê-cê-maka" is a cradle song collected in the state of Mato Grosso among the Parecís Indians. "Nozani-Na," of the same origin, is an example of Amerindian music. "Papá Corumiassú," another cradle song from the state of Pará, has a charming lyricism. The following two songs are recollections of fetichist African *macumbas:* "Xangô," dramatic and rhythmic, and "Estrela é Lua Nova" ("That Star Is a New Moon"), lively and effective. "Viola Quebrada" ("Broken Guitar") is a romantic rural song, "Tu passaste por êste jardim" ("You Have Been in This Garden"), a delightful urban song of the nineties, and "Cabocla do Caxangá," a lively and gay *embolada.* Those who wish to study Brazilian songs should, by all means, start with this valuable collection by Villa-Lobos.

Many musicologists and singers, however, prefer the *Serestas* ("Serenades") as the masterpiece of the Brazilian *lied.* The word *seresta* here stands for all folkloric manifestations and not just those urban serenades typical of Rio at the turn of the century. Written in Paris, between 1925 and

1926, on poems of different modern poets, the series is an authentic anthology of Brazilian song, selected by the experienced Viola-Lobos, who traveled so much to collect them when he was a young man. Although they were composed in a popular manner they are all original creations of the author, who did, however, use some harmonic, melodic, and rhythmic elements drawn from the musical folklore of Brazil. The series begins with "Pobre Cega" ("Poor Blind Woman"), emotional and sad, and continues with "Anjo da Guarda" ("Guardian Angel") and "Canção da Folha Morta" ("Song of the Dead Leaf"), authentic serenades by their melodic line. "Modinha," based on the old Italian aria, is very representative of this type of romantic song. It has an intense lyricism, in spite of its sinuous melody, and a slight touch of the ironic. The next, "Na Paz do Outono" ("In Autumn's Peace"), is one of the most richly descriptive of the Brazilian landscape. One can hear the dripping of autumn raindrops through luxuriant tropical vegetation. "A Cantiga do Viuvo" ("The Widower's Song") is less interesting, but the series reaches a new high in the "Canção do Carreiro" ("Song of the Ox-cart Driver"). Composed in D minor in a first version, the final version is in C major, with changes in the cowpoke's call, first ascending and then descending. The revised edition eliminates a large part of Ribeiro Couto's poem, substituting it by the onomatopoeic syllables *na, na* and *la, la* and omitting several glissandi which overburdened the interpretation. This is a most effective but difficult song. "Abril" ("April") and "Desejo" ("Wish") both contain exquisite freshness, and "Redondilha," a serenade, closes the collection with an ironically sentimental portrait of the backwoodsman.

It was not until 1933 that Villa-Lobos wrote other significant vocal works: *Modinhas e Canções* ("Songs and Serenades"), this time mere harmonizations of well-known popular melodies. Among the most important were the beautiful "Nhapopê," with its rich piano accompaniment, the gallant "Lundú da Marquesa de Santos," the delicate "A Gatinha Parda" ("The Dark Cat") and the dramatic "O Rei Mandou me Chamar" ("The King Sent for Me"), all in the repertoire of every concert singer specializing in Brazilian music.[1]

In the comments on the *Bachiana No. 5,* mention was made of the enormous success of the aria, written in 1938, which is so familiar to the American music lover. Here it is pertinent to point out that the *Bachiana No. 5* is available only in an edition for voice and eight cellos. Another important song for baritone voice and orchestra is "Itabira," dedicated to Marian Anderson, and also very difficult to sing. It is a dramatic piece written in a universal language although well impregnated with Brazilian emotion because of its powerful text.

Villa-Lobos composed over one hundred songs, as usual of very uneven quality. The "Classical Samba" and a few songs with lyrics by Dora Vasconcellos, with whom he was closely associated in New York during his long visits there, may be considered the most attractive works in his last fifteen years of production. Although imperfect and uneven, Villa-Lobos' songs would in themselves be enough to immortalize him.

He was never persistent in composing operas. He wrote many, but none was a success. He first tried his hand at this kind of music in 1912, when some of his enemies had doubted his ability to write an opera. As mentioned before, he composed two one-act operas, *Aglaia* and *Eliza,* which were later enlarged into an ambitious four-act opera called *Izath.* In 1918 the last act of this was staged, and found some public favor. It is a youthful work. The action occurs in Paris, and deals with a ballerina who runs into trouble with Montmartre bandits; some of the music has a gypsy flavor. This opera was not presented in its entirety until 1940, when it achieved only a *succès d'estime.*

By 1921 Villa-Lobos, had already written three more operas: *Jesus* (1918), *Zoe* (1919), and *Malazarte* (1921). The second tells the story of a mulatto Salome in a rather scan-

1. The lundú was a popular song in the early nineteenth century and is probably of African origin. The Marquesa de Santos was a famous mistress of Emperor Pedro I of Brazil.

dalous libretto. The protagonist dies in a dramatic scene, under the effects of morphine, while her lover plays a wild *maxixe* on the piano. "The Infernal Dance" of the second act is published and is an effective piece. *Malazarte*, the story of a popular romantic hero of Brazil, is in the style of the *Cirandas* and *Serestas*. None of these operas was performed.

Written in New York between January and March of 1947, the operetta *Magdalena* is a crazy quilt of the best Villa-Lobos themes. It was produced in New York and in Los Angeles with moderate success; but in all justice to the composer, it must be said that the libretto could not have been worse. It starts in Paris and ends in a vague country in the Andes, with a very commonplace plot bad enough to drag down any music composed for it. In 1956 Villa-Lobos wrote the opera *Yerma,* based on the famous García Lorca play, which at this writing has not yet been performed. The libretto is in English, a language which the composer could set to music only with a great difficulty. In 1957-58 he composed a comic opera in three acts called *A Menina nas Nuvens* ("The Girl in the Clouds"), which likewise has not been performed.

A note is necessary on several religious works of considerable importance: the oratorios *Vida Pura* ("Pure Life") composed in 1918 for mixed chorus, organ, and orchestra; and *Saint Sebastian* (1937) for chorus *a cappella*. Even though they do not merit a high place among Villa-Lobos' works, both oratorios have moments of grandeur in spite of being rather antiliturgical. A *Magnificat Alleluia* for orchestra, mixed chorus, and soloists, with text from the Bible, was composed in 1958 at the request of the Vatican. It was performed on November 8, 1958, by the Brazilian Symphony Orchestra with great success and it seems to be the last significant piece composed by the musician before his death in the following year. Typical Brazilian lyricism flows effectively in the chorus at the finale.

A special reference to Villa-Lobos' choral works is also indispensable. He always strove to improve musical education in Brazil through choral singing, and in his *Practica*

Guide may be found several effective choral pieces which have become quite popular: "O Canto do Pajé" ("The Chief's Song") for four voices, "As Costureiras" ("The Seamstresses") for feminine chorus *a cappella,* and the excellent "Bazzum" for mixed chorus, also *a cappella.*

Villa-Lobos used the chorus in his compositions with great effectiveness; his truly remarkable ability in this respect is evident in such works as the *Chôro No. 10,* the *Brazilian Bachiana No. 9,* the oratorios, *Noneto, Quatuor,* and *Mandú Sarará.*

12 / Homage to Villa-Lobos

... PROBABLY IT WILL BE A TASK for a future generation to make an accurate and reasonable evaluation of the music of Villa-Lobos. Even musicologists of our times have difficulty in reaching a consensus on the whole of his works, due to the differences in style and to the surprises that his fantastic imagination conceived day in day out. Villa-Lobos was perhaps one of the most sincere and artistically honest composers of all times.

LAURINDO ALMEIDA

No sooner had I discovered his music than Villa-Lobos became a musician who had my infinite respect. In our day, when so little music is genuinely or sincerely motivated, when so little music has the quality of spontaneity of expression, it was for me a pleasure to meet an artist with all these qualities, and with the technical mastery as well, which enabled him to express himself in his own language.

As a fellow cellist, his excellent works composed for the instrument, awakened in me a special enthusiasm, and Brazil can take pride in its musical son who bequeathed to the world a music so rich and beautiful.

JOHN BARBIROLLI

I have no words to show my respect for the memory of Villa-Lobos. He was not only a great composer, but also a great Brazilian and an eminent personality of the world artistic community. His works reflect and preserve forever a happy combination of the elements of folklore with the conventional international process of musical creation and he did this in a way that dignifies his country and his art.

LEONARD BERNSTEIN

As the conductor who more often than any other performs his works, I have been studying Villa-Lobos scores daily, and therefore I have learned to respect his memory. Outside of Brazil, I first conducted a Villa-Lobos work with the Boston Symphony Orchestra, in 1946. That piece was already known to Bostonians since Serge Koussevitsky had already presented it. I refer to *Chôro No. 10.* I have conducted Villa-Lobos' music throughout the United States always with great success. The same has happened in Europe, Africa and the Middle East. Today I sincerely regret not to have been an intimate friend of Villa-Lobos. On United Nations Day 1959, one month before his death, I conducted the New York Philharmonic at the General Assembly, and in this concert we played *The Discovery of Brazil* which was hailed by the representatives of all the nations.

ELEAZAR DE CARVALHO

The world of music is indebted to this genial composer not only for his music, but also for his attitude of courage in opposing the subversive currents of what is known today as modern music.

Villa-Lobos followed the precepts of true music and enriched it with the imprint of his strong personality.

Villa-Lobos will remain one of the great figures in the music of his age and one of the greatest glories of the country of his birth.

His example of probity and conscience has not been followed: all the more reason to admire and love it.

PABLO CASALS

"The Hillybilly Train" is one of the most beautiful and most imaginative works by Hector Villa-Lobos. We admire it so much we have recorded it twice, most recently with the New York Philharmonic and all its members. One of my unforgettable souvenirs of Villa-Lobos is connected with a visit that I paid him, on a rainy day, in Paris. We both had colds but our enthusiasm for the piece that Villa-Lobos was playing for me was so great that we both forgot our colds, and in fact the whole world.

ANDRÉ KOSTELANETZ

Villa-Lobos visited Boston on several occasions, before I had come here, to conduct the Boston Symphony Orchestra. He was an excellent conductor, with the authority and sensitivity essential to the great musician he actually was.

The highest moment in my relations with Heitor Villa-Lobos came in 1955 and 1956. To commemorate the 75th Anniversary of the Boston Symphony Orchestra, we were able to commission works from composers throughout the world. Some were young American composers. Others were older European composers. Heitor Villa-Lobos was not only the greatest Brazilian composer, but one of the world's greatest composers. His return to Boston to conduct the first performance of his *11th Symphony* was one of the great moments of our history, and a high point in our personal relationship.

CHARLES MUNCH

A generous, violent nature, of a paradoxal mobility, he creates works in his own image. Without yet attaining an incomparable mastery, or the incredible orchestral virtuosity of the *Chôro No. 8* for example, the *Chôro No. 10* or the Amazon, his *First Symphony,* written in 1916, presages them. The composer denies neither classical form nor the four traditional divisons.

He does not blush to have recourse to the artifices of counterpoint, imitation, fugal exposition, as in the scherzo. How we prefer him in the works which, abandonning himself to his astonishing verve, to his stormy temperament, an irresistable need compels him to express himself freely, in all his fantasy. Thus, he embraces a rhythm, a motif, an idea or a synthesis which his inspiration his creative energy renders fertile: *Serestas, Chôros.*

FLORENT SCHMITT
(Le Temps, 12/28/29)

Heitor Villa-Lobos was one of the greatest composers of the twentieth century because he was able to express, through his music, the immense diversity of life in Brazil, his native country. His music is understood, moreover, by people in many countries, because it is universal. If music burst from him with such spontaneity, it was because he was innately a composer, and extremely prolific. The world of music has been enriched by his works.

LEOPOLD STOKOWSKI

To speak of Villa-Lobos is to recall happy moments of my artistic life. The first recording that I made for Columbia included the *Serestas,* a series of songs by Villa-Lobos, which had been a success in my Town Hall Recitals. That record remains to this day a source of satisfaction and is responsible for many letters of praise from my admirers. I worked with Villa-Lobos with great enthusiasm and constant interest. His approval of important decisions in my career always meant much to me. He will remain in my memory as a special friend and as a sensitive and inspired composer.

JENNIE TOUREL

Bibliographical Note

THERE ARE MANY studies and critical articles on the music of Villa-Lobos, which comment on all aspects of his vast production in various languages. For this bibliography, the reader may wish to consult *A Guide to the Music of Latin America* by Gilbert Chase, published jointly by the Pan American Union and the Library of Congress (Washington, D.C. 1962). The complete catalog of Villa-Lobos' works will be found in *Villa-Lobos, uma Interpretação* by Andrade Muricy (Rio de Janeiro, 1961, in Portuguese) and an almost complete catalog in English is contained in *Composers of the Americas: Biographical Data and Catalogs of their Works* issued by the Music Division of the Pan-American Union (vol. 3, 1957). All other information related to Villa-Lobos may be obtained at the Villa-Lobos Museum, Ministry of Education and Culture, Rio de Janeiro, Brazil (director: Arminda Neves de Almeida).

The following books which deal exclusively with Villa-Lobos' life and works have been published in Portuguese:

BARROS, C. PAULA. *O Romance de Villa-Lobos*. Rio de Janeiro: Ed. A. Noite, 1951.
GIACOMO, ARNALDO MAGALHAES DI. *Villa-Lobos, Alma Sonora do Brasil*. São Paulo, Edicões Melhoramentos, n.d.
Homenagem a Villa-Lobos. Rio de Janeiro: Ministério da Educação e Cultura, 1960.
MARIZ, VASCO. *Heitor Villa-Lobos*. Rio de Janeiro: Ministry of External Relations, 1949.
MURICY, ANDRADE. *Villa-Lobos, uma Interpretação*. Rio de Janeiro: Ministerio da Educacão e Cultura, 1961. Full catalog of works.
Presença de Villa-Lobos (three volumes) by several authors. Rio de Janeiro, Villa-Lobos Museum, 1965, 1966, 1969.
Villa-Lobos, sua obra with a complete catalogue of works and comments by the composer himself. Rio de Janeiro, Villa-Lobos Museum, 1965.
BEAUFILS, MARCEL. *Villa-Lobos, Musicien et Poète du Brésil*. (in French) Paris: Institu des Hautes Études de l'Amérique Latine de l'Universite de Paris, 1967.

The present work has been published in English translation, on June 1963, as No. 24 of *The Latin American Monograph Series* sponsored by the School of Inter-American Studies of the University of Florida, Gainesville, Fla., with preface by Gilbert Chase. A French edition by Pierre Seghers Publishers is listed as No. 31 in the series of books on music entitled *Musiciens de tous les temps* and appeared in Paris in February 1967. The present edition is therefore the fourth of the book written by Vasco Mariz.

There are at least two unpublished biographies of Villa-Lobos, one written in Spanish by the Argentinian art critic Gaston Talamón and the other in German by Swiss musicologist Lisa Peppercorn.

PUBLISHERS AND DISTRIBUTORS OF THE WORKS OF VILLA LOBOS
United States

Associated Music Publishers, Inc. 1 West 47th Street, New York.
Carl Fischer Inc., 62 Cooper Square, New York.
Mercury Music Corporation, 17 West 60th Street, New York.
Ricordi, 16 West 61st Street, New York.
Robbins Music Co. 1350 Avenue of the Americas, New York.
G. Schirmer, Inc., 4 East 49th Street, New York.
Southern Music Publishing Company, 1619 Broadway, New York.

Max Eschig, 30 rue de Rome, Paris, France.
Casa Arthur Napoleão, 46 rua J.P. Duarte, Rio de Janeiro, Brazil.
Irmãos Vitale, 121, rua do Ouvidor, Rio de Janeiro, Brazil.

CHRONOLOGICAL LIST OF IMPORTANT WORKS BY VILLA LOBOS*

Year	Title	Instruments	Publisher
1908–12	Popular Brazilian Suite	Solo Guitar	Max Eschig
1911	Trio No. 1	Piano, violin and cello	Max Eschig
1912	Sonata Fantasia No. 1 (Despair)	Violin and piano	Max Eschig
1913	Izaht	Opera in 4 Acts	Max Eschig
1914–16	African Dances	Piano solo or orchestra	Max Eschig &Ricordi
	Sonata Fantasia No. 2	Violin and piano	Max Eschig
1915	Concerto No. 1	Cello and Orchestra	Max Eschig
	Quartet No. 1	Strings	Southern
	Quartet No. 2	Strings	Max Eschig
1916–17	Miniatures	Voice and piano	Napoleão
1916	Quartet No. 3	Strings	Max Eschig
	Symphony No. 1	Orchestra	Southern
	Sinfonietta No. 1	Chamber Orchestra	Southern
	Sonata No. 2	Cello and piano	Max Eschig
	Trio No. 2	Piano, violin and cello	Max Eschig
1917	Amazon (Ballet)	Orchestra	Max Eschig
	Song of the Black Swan	Violin and piano	Napoleão
	Quartet No. 4	Strings	Associated
	Symphony No. 2	Orchestra	Ricordi
	Floral Suite	Piano solo	Napoleão
	Uirapuru (ballet)	Orchestra	Associated

Year	Title	Instruments	Publisher
1918	Prole do Bébe (the Baby Family)	Piano solo	Napoleão
	Trio No. 3	Piano, violin and cello	Max Eschig
1919	Canções tipicas brasileiras (Typical Brazilian Songs)	Voice and piano	Max Eschig
	Carnival of the Brazilian Children Children Piano solo	Piano solo	Napoleão
	Symphony No. 3	Orchestra and fanfare	Ricordi
	Symphony No. 4	Orchestra and fanfare	Ricordi
	Vidapura	Oratorio	Ricordi
	Zoe	Opera in three acts	Ricordi
1920	Choros No. 1	Solo Guitar	Napoleão
	Historietas (in French)	Voice and piano	Napoleão
	Lenda do Caboclo	Piano solo	Napoleão
	Sonata No. 3	Violin and piano	Napoleão
	Symphony No. 3	Orchestra, chorus and fanfare	Max Eschig
1921	The Spinner	Piano solo	Napoleão
	Malazarte	Opera in 3 Acts	Napoleão
	Prole do Bebé No. 2	Piano solo	Max Eschig
	Quartet	Harp, celeste, flute saxophone and women's choir	Max Eschig
	Trio	Oboe, clarinet and bassoon	Max Eschig
1922	Fantasia of Mixed Movements	Violin and piano Violin and orchestra	Southern
1923	Noneto	Flute, oboe, clarinet, saxophone, bassoon, celeste, harp, percussion and chorus	Max Eschig
1923-26	Rudepoema	Piano or orchestra	Max Eschig
1923	Suite for Voice and Violin	Voice and violin	Max Eschig
	Sonata No. 4	Violin and piano	Max Eschig
1924	Choros No. 2	Flute and clarinet (piano reduction)	Napoleão
	Choros No. 7	Flute, oboe, clarinet alto saxophone, bassoon, tamtam, violin and cello	
1925	Choros No. 3	Clarinet, saxophone, bassoon, trumpet, trombone, and mens chorus	Max Eschig
	Choros No. 8	2 Pianos and orchestra	Max Eschig
	Choros No. 10	Orchestra and mixed Choir	Max Eschig
	The Martyrdom of the Insects	Violin and Piano, Violin and Orchestra	Associated
	Serestas (Serenades)	Voice and piano, or Voice and orchestra	Napoleão & Max Eschig

Year	Title	Instruments	Publisher
1926	Choros No. 4	3 trumpets and trombone	Max Eschig
	Choros No. 5	Piano solo	Max Eschig
	Choros No. 6	Orchestra	Max Eschig
	Cirandas	Piano solo	Napoleão
1927	Saudades das Selvas Brasileiras (Soùvenir of the Brazilian Jungle)	Piano solo	Max Eschig
1928	Choros Bis	Violin and cello	Max Eschig
		Piano and orchestra	Associated
	Choros No. 11	Reduction for 2 pianos	Associated
	Choros No. 14	Orchestra, fanfare and Choir	Associated
	Quartet	Flute, oboe, clarinet and saxophone	Max Eschig
	Quintet	Flute, oboe, clarinet, English Horn, bassoon	Max Eschig
1929	Choros No. 9	Orchestra	Max Eschig
	Choros No. 12	Orchestra	Associated
	Choros No. 13	2 Orchestras & fanfare	Associated
	Francette and Pia	Piano solo	Max Eschig
	Introduction to Choros	Orchestra	Associated
	Momo Precoce	Piano and orchestra	Max Eschig
	Suite Suggestive (in French)	Voice and Piano	Max Eschig
1930	Bachianas Brasileiras No. 1	Eight celli	Associated
	Bachianas No. 2	Orchestra	Associated
	Bahcianas No. 4	Piano solo	Associated
1931	Quartet No. 5	Strings	Associated
1932	Caixinha de Boas Festas	Orchestra	Ricordi
	The Seamstresses	Women voices	Schirmer
	Guide Pratique (Eleven albums)	Piano solo Vitate Max Eschig	Consolidated Mercury Southern
1933	Ciranda des Sept Notes	Bassoon and strings	Southern
1933–42	Modinhas and Songs	Voice and Piano or Orchestra	Max Eschig
1936	Bazzum	Mens voices	Max Eschig
	Brazilian Cycle	Piano solo	Napoleão
1937	The Discovery of Brazil	Orchestra (4 Suites)	Max Eschig
	Mass of San Sebastian	Choir for 3 voices	Associated
1938	Bachianas No. 3	Piano and Orchestra	Ricordi
	Bachianas No. 5	Voice and Orchestra	Associated
	Bachianas No. 6	Flute and bassoon	Associated
	Quartet No. 6	Strings	Associated
1939	New York Skyline Melody	Orchestra or piano	Max Eschig
	Mandu Sarara (ballet)	Orchestra, Choir and percussion	Max Eschig
	Six preludes	Guitar solo	Max Eschig
	The Three Maries	Piano solo	Fischer

Year	Title	Instruments	Publisher
1942	Bachianas No. 7	Orchestra	Max Eschig
	Itabira	Orchestra, base or contralto and Orchestra or piano	Max Eschig
	Poema Singelo (Simple Poem)	Piano solo	Vitale
	Quartet No. 7	Strings	Associated
1942	Invocation in Defense of the Fatherland	Womens voices, soperano and Orchestra	Max Eschig
	Modinhas and Songs (Second collection)	Voice and Piano	Max Eschig
1944	Bachianas No. 8	Orchestra	Max Eschig
	Quartet No. 8	Strings	Ricordi
	Symphony No. 6	Orchestra	Ricordi
1945	Songs of Cordiality	Choir, 2,3,4 Voices	Ricordi
	Bachianas No. 9	A cappella Choir or Orchestra	Max Eschig
	Concerto No. 1	Piano and orchestra	Associated
	Fantasia	Cello and orchestra	Associated
	Madonna	Orchestra	Associated
	Quartet No. 9	Strings	Associated
	Symphony No. 7	Orchestra	Associated
	Trio	Violin, viola and cello	Max Eschig
	Duo	Violin and viola	Mercury
1946	Two Landscapes	Voice and piano	Max Eschig
	Quartet No. 10	Strings	Southern
	Digression	Cello, piano and tam-tam	Max Eschig
1947	Magdelena	Opera in two acts	Max Eschig
	Sinfonietta No. 2	Orchestra	Southern
1948	Big Ben (English)	Orchestra and Voice	Southern
	Fantasia	Saxophone, strings & 2 trumpets	Southern
	Quartet No. 11	Strings	
1949	Homage to Chopin	Piano solo	Max Eschig
1950	Symphony No. 8	Orchestra	Max Eschig
	Erosion	Orchestra	Max Eschig
	Classical Samba	Voice and Piano or Orchestra	Max Eschig
	Quartet No. 12	Strings	Southern
	Quartet No. 13	Strings	Southern
1951	Concerto	Guitar and orchestra or piano	Max Eschig
	Symphony No. 9	Orchestra	Max Eschig
	Ruda (ballet)	Orchestra	Ricordi
1952	Concerto No. 4	Piano and orchestra	Associated
	Symphony No. 10	Soloists, choir and orchestra	Max Eschig

Year	Title	Instruments	Publisher
1953	Fantasia Concertante	Piano, clarinet and bassoon	Max Eschig
	Concerto	Harp and orchestra	Associated
	Alvoreda na Floresta Tropical (Dawn in the Tropical Forest)	Orchestra	Max Eschig
	Quartet No. 14	Strings	Max Eschig
	Odyssey of a Race	Orchestra	Israel
	Concerto No. 2	Cello and orchestra	Associated
1954	Concerto No. 5	Piano and orchestra	Associated
	Quartet No. 15	Strings	
1955	Symphony No. 11	Orchestra	Associated
	Quartet No. 16	Strings	Associated
	Concerto	Mouth harmonica and orchestra	Associated
1956	Yerma	Opera in 3 acts	Associated
	Emperor Jones (ballet)	Orchestra and baritone and soprano solos	Associated
	Symphony No. 12	Orchestra	Associated
1957	Duo	Oboe and bassoon	Max Eschig
	Quintet	Piano and orchestra	Max Eschig
		Flute, harp, violin, viola and cello	Max Eschig
	Quartet No. 17	Strings	Max Eschig
1958	Girl in the Clouds	Comic opera in 3 acts	Max Eschig
	Bendita Sabedoria (Blessed Wisdom)	Choir for 6 voices	Max Eschig
	Fantasia Concertante	Orchestra of celli	Max Eschig
	Magnificat Alleluia	Orchestra, mixed voices and solo	Max Eschig
	Sailing Boats (Veleiros)	Voice and orchestra piano	Robbins
	Song of the Tropical Forest	Orchestra, mens choir and solo	Max Eschig
	Concerto Grosso	Flute, oboe, clarinet and bassoon	Peters

* A complete list of the works of Heitor Villa-Lobos would number approximately one thousand.

Discography

The following villa-lobos recordings are available in the United States.

THE CHOROS

* CHORO No. 1 for Guitar. Julian Bream, guitar. RCA Victor LSC-2606.-José Luis Gonzalez, guitar, Odyssey 32160200 - Oyanguren, guitar. Decca 8018.

* CHORO No. 5 ("Alma Brasileira") for Piano. Charles Milgrim, Dança. do indio branco, Choros only. Crossroads 22160113-2216014.

BRAZILIAN BACHIANAS

* BACHIANAS BRASILEIRAS No. 1 for 8 Celli. Concert Arts Orchestra, Felix Slatkin, Conductor. Capital (S) P-8484—New York Stadium Symphony, Leopold Stokowski, Conductor (Modinha only), Everest 3061.

* BACHIANAS BRASILEIRAS No. 2 for Orchestra. Orchestre National de la Radiodiffusion française, Heitor Villa-Lobos, Conductor. Angel 35547.

* BACHIANAS BRASILEIRAS No. 3 for Piano and Orchestra. Trieste Philharmonic Orchestra, Felicia Blumenthal, piano, Luigi Toffolo, Conductor. VOX 10070.

* BACHIANAS BRASILEIRAS No. 4 for Orchestra. Orchestre National de la Radiodiffusion Francaise, Heitor Villa-Lobos, Conductor. Angel 35547.

* BACHIANAS BRASILEIRAS No. 5 for Soprano and 8 Celli. Joan Baez, Vanguard (7) 9160.—Nethania Devrath, soprano, New York Philharmonic, Leonard Bernstein, Conductor, Columbia MS-6514—Victoria de los Angeles, soprano, Orchestre National de la Radiodiffusion Française, Heitor Villa-Lobos, Conductor, Angel 35547—Anna Moffo, soprano, American Symphony Orchestra, Leopold Stokowski, Conductor, RCA Victor LSC—2795—Marni Nixon, soprano, Concert Arts Cello Ensemble, Felix Slatkin, Con-

ductor Capitol (S) P-8484—Renzi, soprano, Carlos Surinach, Conductor, Port. Ensemble, Heliodor (S)25037—Bidu Sayão, Soprano, 8 celli and bass (Aria only), Heitor Villa-Lobos, Conductor, Columbia ML-5231—Sally Terri, soprano, Laurindo Almeida, guitar, Capitol P-8406.—Galina Vishnevskaya, soprano. Rostropovich, cello. Artia 157.

* BACHIANAS BRASILEIRAS No. 6 for Flute and Bassoon. Samuel Baron, flute, Bernard Garfield, bassoon. Nonesuch 71030—Samuel Baron, flute, Weisberg, bassoon, Concert-disc 254—Boston Symphony Chamber Players, RCA Victor LM/LSC-6184—Fernand Dufrene, flute, Rene Plessier, bassoon, Angel 35547.

* BACHIANAS BRASILEIRAS No. 7 for Strings. Orchestre National de la Radiodiffusion Française, Heitor Villa-Lobos, Conductor. Angel 35674.

* BACHIANAS BRASILEIRAS No. 9 for Strings. Orchestre National de la Radiodiffusion Française, Heitor Villa-Lobos, Conductor. Angel 35547.

MUSIC FOR ORCHESTRA

* CONCERTO No. 2 for Cello & Orchestra. Aldo Parisot, cello, Orchestra of the Vienna State Opera, Gustav Meier, Conductor. Westminster-19037.

* CONCERTO for Guitar & Orchestra. Laurindo Almeida, guitar, Wilson Concert Arts Chamber Orchestra, Capitol (S)P-8638.

* CONCERTO for Mouth Harmonica & Orchestra. John Sebastian, harmonica, Schwieger, Conductor, Stuttgart Symphony Orchestra. Heliodor S-25064.

* FANTASIA CONCERTANTE for Orchestra of Cellos. Violincello Society Orchestra—32 cellis. Heitor Villa-Lobos, Conductor. Everest (stereo) 3024.

* ALVORADA NA FLORESTA TROPICAL (Dawn in the Tropical Forest). Louisville Symphony Orchestra. Robert Whitney, Conductor. Louisville 545-1.

* THE FOREST OF THE AMAZON. Symphony of the Air, Bidu Sayão, soprano, Heitor Villa-Lobos, Conductor. United Artists 8007.

* LITTLE TRAIN OF THE CAIPIRA (from Bachianas No. 2). London Symphony Orchestra, Eugène Gooseens, Conductor. Everest 3041.—Morton Gould, Conductor. RCA Victor LM/LSC-

1994.—Grunke Symphony Orchestra (coll. Impressionisiu in Art & Music) Buena Vista (S)-4040.—Howard Mitchell, conductor, National Symphony Orchestra, RCA Victor LSC-2813.

* ORIGIN OF THE AMAZON RIVER, Robert Whitney, Conductor, Louisville Symphony Orchestra. Columbia CML-4615.

* UIRAPURU. New York Stadium Symphony, Leopold Stokowski Conductor. Everest 3016.

CHAMBER MUSIC

* QUINTETTE EN FORME DE CHOROS. New York Woodwind Quintet, Nonesuch 71030.

* TRIO FOR OBOE, CLARINET, BASSOON; QUARTET FOR FLUTE, OBOE, CLARINET & BASSOON; QUINTET FOR FLUTE, OBOE, ENGLISH HORN, CLARINET & BASSOON. New Art Wind Quintet. Westminster 9071.

* QUARTET No. 17. Brazilian Orchestra, Nepomuceno. Odyssey 32160176.

MUSIC FOR PIANO

* PROLE DO BEBÊ, SUITES No. 1 & 2. José Echaniz, Westminster 9343.—Charles Milgrim, Crossroads 22160114—Artur Rubinstein (Suites 1-6) RCA VICTOR LSC-2605.

* RUDEPOEMA—Bean, RCA Victor-1379.

MUSIC FOR GUITAR

* FIVE PRELUDES FOR GUITAR. Julian Bream, Westminster-14983.

VOCAL MUSIC

* CANÇÕES TIPICAS BRASILEIRAS. Phyllis Curtin, Vanguard-1125.

The following is a list of Villa-Lobos recordings available in Europe and Latin America.

THE CHOROS

* CHORO No. 1 for Guitar Heitor Villa-Lobos, guitar, RCA Victor 12 204 (Brazil).—Alirio Diaz, guitar. La Boite à Musique BAMLD 032 (France).

* CHORO No. 2 for Flute and Clarine. Fernand Dufrene, flute and Maurice Cliquetois, clarinet. La Voix de son Maitre (FALP 596-597 (France).

* CHORO No. 3 for Clarinet, Saxophone, Bassoon, Violin and men's choir. R. Siohan, Conductor. GW 914 (France).

* CHORO No. 5 (for Piano solo) Ellen Ballon, Decca M 671 (Great Britain)—Arnaldo Estrella, Le Chant du Monde (France). Aline van Barentzen, La Voix de son Maitre FALP 596-597 (France).

* CHORO No. 10 (Choir and Orchestra). Orchestre National de la Radiodiffusion Française. Chorale des Jeunesses Musicales, Heitor Villa-Lobos, Conductor. Columbia FCX 602-603 (France).

* CHORO No. 11 (Piano and Orchestra). Orchestre National de la Radiodiffusion Française. Aline van Barentzen, piano. Conductor, Heitor Villa-Lobos. La Voix de son Maitre FALP 596-597 (France).

* CHORO BIS (Violin and Cello). H. Bronschawak, Violin and J. Neitz, cello, Columbia FCX 668 (France).

BRAZILIAN BACHIANAS

* BACHIANAS BRASILEIRAS No. 1 (for 8 Celli). Ensemble of 24 celli. Heitor Villa-Lobos, Conductor. La Voix de son Maitre FALP 596-597 (France).

* BACHIANAS BRASILEIRAS No. 2 (for Orchestra). Orchestre National de la Radiodiffusion Française. Heitor Villa-Lobos, Conductor. La Voix de son Maitre (FALP) 476 (France).

* BACHIANAS BRASILEIRAS No. 3 (Piano and Orchestra).—Orchestre National de la Radiodiffusion Française, Manuel Antonio Braune, piano. Heitor Villa-Lobos, Conductor. Columbia Masterworks FCX 668 A (France).

* BACHIANAS BRASILEIRAS No. 4 (Piano solo). Gilberto Tinetti, piano, Chantecler CMG 1 018 (Brazil).—(Orchestral version), Orchestre National de la Radiodiffusion Française, Heitor Villa-Lobos, Conductor, Columbia FCX 667 A (France).

* BACHIANAS BRASILEIRAS No. 5 (Soprano and 8 Celli), Federo Aleman, soprano, Pedro Rios Reyna, Conductor. SAM Caracas XTV 26 887 (Venezuela).—Alice Ribeiro, Soprano, José Siqueira, Conductor. Le Chant du Monde 8 119 (France).

* BACHIANAS BRASILEIRAS No. 6 (for Flute and Bassoon).

Jacques Castagner, flute and Gerard Faisandier, bassoon. Vega C 35 A 140 (France).

MUSIC FOR ORCHESTRA

* CONCERTO No. 1 (for Piano and Orchestra). Orchestre National de la Suisse Romande. Ellen Ballon, piano. London 11 77 (Great Britiain).

* CONCERTO No. 5 (for Cello and Orchestra). Orchestre National de la Radiodiffusion Française. Heitor Villa-Lobos, Conductor. Felicia Blumenthal, pianist. Columbia FOX 438 (France).

* THE DISCOVERY OF BRAZIL (4 Suites). Grand Prix du Disque of Paris. Orchestre National de la Radiodiffusion Francaise. Heitor Villa-Lobos, Conductor. Columbia FCX 602-603 (France).

* INVOCATION IN DEFENSE OF THE FATHERLAND. Orcheste Nationale de la Radiodiffusion Française. Chorale of the French Jeunesses Musicales. Heitor Villa-Lobos, Conductor. Columbia FCX 602-603 (France).

* MAGNIFICAT ALLELUIA. Choral Association of Rio de Janeiro. Brazilian Symphony. Orchestra, Eduardo de Guarnieri, Conductor. Festa LDR 5 020 (Brazil).

CHAMBER MUSIC

* QUARTET No. 5. Quarteto Carioca. Victor 11 212—11 213 Victor (Brazil).

* QUARTET No. 11. Official Quartet of the National School of Music. Columbia Masterworks 6 041 (Brazil).

CHORAL MUSIC

* BENDITA SABEDORIA (Blessed Wisdom). Choral Association of Rio de Janeiro. Cleofe Person de Matos, Conductor. Festa LDR 5 025 (Brazil).

MUSIC FOR PIANO

* PROLE DO BEBÊ. Suite No. 1 (The Baby's Family). Aline Van Barentzen, La Voix de son Maitre FALP 417. (France). Magda Tagliaferro. (Polichinelle, only) Ducretet Thomson DTLP 400 020 (France).—Ellen Ballon (Polichinelle, only) Decca 512 & London LS 531 (Great Britain).

* PROLE DO BEBÉ, Suite No. 2. Aline Van Barentzen, La Voix de son Maitre FALP 417 (France).

* GUIDE PRATIQUE. Roberto Szidon, Angel 3 CDX 401-402 (Brazil).

* BRAZILIAN CYCLE. (3 pieces). Anna Stella Schic, Le Chant du Monde LDX 8 004 (France).—Elizabeth Powell, RCS 22 (Great Britain).—Magda Tagliaferro, Ducretet Thomson DTLP 40 020 France).

* IMPRESSION DE SERENADE (Impressões Seresteiras—from the Brazilian Cycle). Ellen Ballon, London LD 9 095 (Great Britain).

* DANCE OF THE WHITE INDIAN (Dança do Indio Branco—from the Brazilian Cycle). Homero Magalhães, Decca 163 580 (France).

* LENDA DO CABOCLO. Elizabeth Powell, RCS 22 (Great Britain).

* RUDE POÈME. Roberto Szidon, Angel S 3 CBX 385 stereo (Brazil).

* SAUDADES DAS SELVAS BRASILEIRAS (Remembrance of the Brazilian Forests). Homero Magalhães, Supraphon SUK 36 081 (Checkoslovakia) Same edition available in France (Decca 163 850).

MUSIC FOR GUITAR

* ETUDE No. 1. Andre Segovia, Decca DL 9 638 (Great Britain)—Alirio Diaz, France MAM LD 032 (France).—John Williams, Delyse Recording Co. ECP 3 149 (Great Britain).

* ETUDE No. 7.—Alirio Diaz, BAM LD 053 (France).—Andre Segovia, Deutsche Gramophon 19 051 (Germany).

* 12 ETUDES FOR GUITAR. Turibio dos Santos, Caravelle LP CAR 43 001 (Brazil).

* PRELUDE No. 3. Andre Segovia, Deutsche Gramophon LPEM 19 152 (Germany).

* CONCERTO FOR GUITAR & ORCHESTRA. São Paulo Symphony Orchestra, Maria Livia São Marcos, guitar. Armando Belardi, Conductor. Audio Fidelity, 1 991 (Brazil).

VOCAL MUSIC

* SERESTAS. (entire series) Maria de Lourdes Cruz Lopes, soprano. Odeon MOFB 3 313 (Brazil).

* CANÇÃO DO CARREIRO. Gerard Souzay, baritone. La Voix

de son Maitre (Stereo) ASDF 242 (France).—Maria Kareska, soprano. Ducretet Thomson (France).

* CANÇÕES TIPICAS BRASILEIRAS. (entire series) Cristina Maristany, soprano and Alceu Bocchino, piano. Angel 3 CBX 395 (Brazil).

* XANGO. Gerard Souzay, baritone. La Voix de son Maitre (stereo)—ADSF 242 (France).

* CANTILENA ET VIOLA. Frederick Fulter, tenor, Heitor Villa Lobos, piano. His Master Voice (Great Britain).

* MODINHAS ET CHANSONS (Album No. 1 & 2). Entire series. Lia Salgado, soprano, Murilo Santos, piano. Caravelle 43 004 (Brazil).

* THREE INDIGENOUS POEMS. Andino Abreu, baritone. GP 761 (France).